Healing The Wounds
of
Change

Healing The Wounds of Change

Steps Toward Personal and Spiritual Renewal

Anne M. Brady Reinsmith

Copyright © 2012 by Anne M. Brady Reinsmith.

ISBN: Softcover   978-1-4797-2714-8
       Ebook   978-1-4797-2715-5

All rights reserved. No part of this book may be reproduced or transmitted in any form or by any means, electronic or mechanical, including photocopying, recording, or by any information storage and retrieval system, without permission in writing from the copyright owner.

All names and case incidents have been fictionalized to protect the privacy of those involved. The New Testament Scripture quotes in this volume are taken from the *New Testament in Modern English*, revised edition, by J.B. Phillips, 1972. The Old Testament Scriptural references are taken from *The Holy Bible, New* Revised Standard Version, 1989.

The information in this volume is not intended as a substitute for consultation with a qualified professional.

This book was printed in the United States of America.

To order additional copies of this book, contact:
Xlibris Corporation
1-888-795-4274
www.Xlibris.com
Orders@Xlibris.com
123374

Dedication
This book is dedicated to
Peggy and Jackie
whose enduring courage and compassionate love
have given clear witness
to God's faithful presence, within, among, and beyond us.

ACKNOWLEDGEMENTS

This book owes its genesis and "birth," in large part, to those educators and mentors whose works have contributed to the understanding and appreciation of the complex process involved in our personal, spiritual well-being. To them, and to my family, friends, and acquaintances who have encouraged and supported my efforts to publish this book, I am most thankful. To my advisors at Xlibris who have guided me through the publishing process, and to those who will read this book in order to renew their efforts to "change your mind and heart and believe the good news," to each and all, I offer my sincere thanks. My deepest appreciation for all the behind-the-scenes support goes to Bill, who so generously and faithfully gave his time and expertise as I made my way through the ups-and-downs of completing this book.

Contents

1. Understand the Significance of Change 17
   The Meaning and Value of Change. 17
   The Danger of Sameness 19
   Change as an Attachment Challenge. 20
   The Now of Change. 23
   Spirituality and Change. 26

2. Know the Many Faces of Change 33
   Change in Its Different Forms 33
   Aging with Grace 36
   Death and Dignity 39
   Acknowledging Feelings of Pain 41
   Dealing Effectively with Change 45

3. Get Beyond the Stress of Change 51
   Stress as an Integral Part of Change 51
   Spirituality and Stress Control 55
   Busyness, an Occupational Hazard 58
   Healing the Wounds of Change 60
   Gifts of Change 64

4. Appreciate the Relational Nature of Change 68
   Treasured Remembrances of Solidarity 68
   Communal Belonging 71
   Getting Stuck in Family Roles 73
   Spirituality and the Elephant Tracks 76
   Everything is Grace 79

5. Move Beyond the Fears and Anxieties of Change 81
   Developmental Challenges of Change.. 81
   Self-Love Without Apology.. 84
   Seeing the Wisdom of Our Discontents... 86
   Legacies of Psychospiritual Change 90
   Truth and Consequences.. 94

6. Access the Psychospiritual Dimensions of Change 97
   Valuing Psychospiritual Change 97
   New Wine and New Wineskins.. 101
   The Human Face of God.. 103
   Discernment and Change-Ability 105
   The Healing Power of Presence 112

7. Begin Holistic Renewal Now 115
   Meeting the Demands of Change 115
   Habits of Renewal 119
   Empowerment Through Spiritual Practice 122
   Revisit the Forgotten Virtues 126
   Spiritual Flourishing... 132

INTRODUCTION

Across the airways of our global village, the information flashes: earthquakes in Haiti, in Japan, in Chile, and beyond. When the ground beneath our feet does not hold firm, panic runs riot. Understandably so! The "shaking of the foundations" affects all earthlings, from the lowest to the highest. And running hardly helps, especially when there is no place to hide.

Another type of "earthquake" causes real fear and trembling for us. Though more subtle, more frequent, and more varied, it too brings anxiety and panic. It too shakes the foundations of the human body, mind, and spirit. This more familiar deep disturbance is known as change. Although it is a necessary part of life, few of us choose to deal with it productively. Even devout Christians who follow willingly the precepts of their faith, find Jesus' mandate a huge challenge: "You must change your minds and hearts and believe the good news." (Mark 1:15).

So what is this fear-inducing, change happening all about? How does it invade our comfort zone? And what can we do about it? These are a few of the concerns we will explore in the following pages, as we focus on the challenges of change, and on the opportunities it allows for personal and spiritual development.

Many years ago I set out to live a meaningful, productive life, a life totally dedicated to God, and to others. How surprised I was to find difficulties, discouragement, and confusion. Even in the best of conditions I found that living my life's goal was not "a piece of cake." The change of mind and heart that Jesus calls us to is not a once and done experience. It is all-encompassing and on-going. New valleys to forge, new mountains to climb, new challenges to meet, all face us at every turn. And the one common denominator of this everyday happening is change! Life's map shows no straight and easy road to transformation, only the winding, climbing, on-going, flux and flow of change.

Except for our own obtuse attitude, our own preferences for platitudinal absolutes, our own backward perspectives, we serious seekers of the meaningful life have little to fear. Many tried and true directives are available. Maybe too many! Having been one of those sincere searchers of the meaningful life, I tried to absorb too much, too fast. My immaturity and idealism left me confused and uncomfortable. C.G. Jung wrote "The psychic depths are nature, and nature is creative life." Happiness and contentment follow in the wake of living creatively, of being open to change, of applying natural talents and capabilities for personal and spiritual advancement. This in turn allows for communal well-being to flourish. But there I was, in my young life, pulled between idealism and reality, between solidarity with others, and autonomy of self. The rack of perfection was stretching me to the breaking point. Before being a mature person, I had to first learn how to be my own person, how to more fully appreciate the systemic connections of my body, mind, spirit capabilities and limitations. This required inclusive thinking, and openness to change.

The scribe who approached Jesus, in Mark 12: 28-34, reminds me of myself, of my stubborn stance against change. I can easily imagine this professional copyist as being impressed by the easy, confident manner of Jesus as he spoke to his listeners. As John P. Meier reminds us, in Jesus' time scribes did not belong to any one group. Their function was to write and copy documents. Like the word "secretary" today, scribe is not easily defined. He could be educationally limited, or educationally advanced. He could be a "pen pusher" or have sophisticated religious knowledge. This particular scribe asked Jesus the direct question, "What are we to consider the greatest commandment of all?" And he got a direct answer. When he acknowledged Jesus' reply, the scribe was assured, "You are not far from the kingdom of God!"

This answer of Jesus puzzled me. Why was the scribe "not far?" Perhaps "not far" meant he needed the level of simplicity and spontaneity that comes with the openness to change? Creative ability, locked away unused, does not serve the inquiring mind and heart. Inspired imaginings must freely engage with matter-of-fact cognition in order for us to really believe the good news, in order for us to experience the fullness of life. The early part of my life's journey found me "not far." But like the scribe, I over-valued those "impressive facts," verbal proofs, and absolute assurances that can so easily lead to egocentric complacency. The challenges of change had much to teach me.

And one of its first lessons, one that I remember vividly, was given during the first few weeks of my high school tenure. In order to be eligible as a school newspaper, or yearbook candidate, Journalism class was a requirement. My grade school grounding in English was above par. The Sisters who taught in our parish school wrote the book on grammar, literally! *Voyages in English* was our "bible" for proper writing. Beginning a sentence with "And" or ending a sentence with a preposition was anathema. My egocentric complacency was pure: I knew all the rules, and then some, and was a bit too proud of the fact. At our first Journalism class our assignment was to critique several newspaper writings. The following week, I was proud to announce my findings: an errant journalist who began a sentence with "And!" Then came a most valuable lesson on change.

Besides having expertise in English, Sister was an accomplished musician. She patiently explained to me that in music, one must learn all the rules. Then, having mastered the rules, one is free to creatively change the timing and harmonies, in order to form new compositions. The journalist had mastered his word-art, he creatively used "And." What was still beyond me, as a young adolescent, was the wisdom to know when and how creative change is called for. But true wisdom comes with the hard work of experience, prayer, detachment, and the realization that all of me (body, mind, and spirit) must be involved in this work of discernment and change. Our Model, Jesus, makes this clear by his own example. Any way you look at it, enhanced living calls for meaningful change of mind and heart.

If you had an opportunity to improve your present situation by making a significant life change, would you? The answer seems easy. But the actual doing is difficult. Why? Change, in any of its forms, remains a huge challenge. We talk freely about the importance of change, about its significance and necessity. But we often hesitate to walk-the-talk of our convictions. For too many of us, change is off-limits, not a topic for casual conversation. It is even less appreciated when we consider the personal and spiritual requirements of change that can assure our total well-being.

Along with the gift of life, we have been given the challenge and opportunity to make our own choices, to open ourselves to the fullness of that Life, "ever ancient, ever new." The gospel mandate to change our minds and hearts, and believe the good news, still holds. But it does not come with a no-conflicts warranty. Instead its implicit message says: You must be open to the creative possibilities of on-going change.

My own adult life relationship with change has been a love-hate affair. I have always enjoyed cooking, but I rarely use the same recipe twice. My preference for trying new combinations of ingredients might label me a "change addict." But when it comes to the personal and spiritual concerns of life, I join the multitudes who prefer the changeless option, the certainty of the well-trod path.

In spite of what might be considered a privileged religious and academic background, I was for a long time, clueless when it came to dealing with change. Whether they came as minimal disappointments, or like tsunami size traumas, change of any kind had me feeling drained of energy, confused in understanding, and aching in emotion. And my Faith? At times it felt like a bucket with a porous bottom, with very little holding power. My being typed on personality inventories as "seeking meaning and connection, being organized, decisive, and committed to firm values" did not improve my relationship with change. It remained an unwelcome challenge!

With the hope of gaining practical insights into the discomfort of change, I began some serious nosing around. The result: Among other things, I found that fears and anxieties about change touch us all, even the most successful professionals, dedicated individuals, and spiritually astute leaders. The dilemma of how to deal with change persists. Even with our honest efforts to deal effectually with these challenges, change remains a formidable stumbling block. Through many decades of trying to meet my own change challenges, and through many years of professional work as educator, psychotherapist, and pastoral counselor, I have come upon several helpful ways to better understand, resolve, and heal the wounds left in the wake of change. For example, I believe with Thomas Merton, that in times of change, fear, and anxiety, we need to trust God, no matter how we feel. Yes, I do most heartily agree! And yet, how do I go about living that holy trust, especially when I am crushed by the overwhelming pain of change? What is it about the human body, mind, spirit holistic relationship, and its connection with God's amazing grace that can empower me to trust in the Divine Presence here and now? No matter what!

More specifically, what does this holistic approach to the healing of our change wounds involve? In general, it involves the whole person, body, mind, and spirit. Experience supports the fact that nature and grace work together as the human developmental process moves toward its purpose: God/Ultimate Reality. This book of observations, clarifications, and reflections underscores the challenge and opportunity to change our minds and hearts and live the fullness of life. To engage in a living Faith, in a full awareness of our purpose and potential, every part of who we are must be involved. Cognition, intuition, and all that makes us human calls us to renewal and transformation, calls us to change.

Healing the Wounds of Change attempts to facilitate personal and spiritual renewal through the experience of change. This involves a deeper understanding and a fuller acceptance of both the psychological and spiritual imperative to change, and our own unique capabilities for that transformation. Using recent, relevant resources, and meaningful spiritual practices, *Healing the Wounds of Change* offers several insights into the possibilities of personal and spiritual renewal. While it is direct, clear, and practical, this book is at the same time profound in its simplicity. It presents a holistic Christian approach for dealing with our challenges of change, and for living a meaningful, productive life.

Healing the Wounds of Change begins with a close-up look at the meaning and value of change, at the challenge it presents at any time, under any circumstances. Because it is a universal phenomenon, we must face it, deal with it. There is no place to hide. It touches every aspect of our lives, both personal and spiritual. Consequently, we do ourselves a great favor by giving serious consideration to its pinches and pokes, to its attachment and separation challenges, to its significance as Jesus' invitation to change and be renewed. (Mark 1:15).

Chapter 2, helps us focus on the many different kinds of change, some very obvious, some more subtle. All quite disturbing; many exceedingly painful! Death loss is only one kind of challenging change, and not necessarily the most crushing. Having the courage to face our change wounds, to deal with them effectually, and to adopt a more inclusive perspective, opens us to possibilities for deep healing. We can then more fully appreciate Jesus' words: "Go home in peace, and be free from your trouble." (Mark 5:34).

Chapter 3, examines the negative effects of stress, and the problems it causes in our personal, and spiritual efforts to live a meaningful, productive life. Real life examples show caring, compassionate individuals who are faced with the burnout syndrome—and discover their change-ability, their capacity for understanding and resolving the stress dilemma. Here we join the ranks of those who continue their persistent asking, searching, and knocking (Luke 11:9) until wisdom and grace bring healing and peace.

Chapter 4, takes us down a familiar path that holds unexpected treasures. Revisiting our relationships with family, friends, and beyond can uncover empowering examples and experiences. From today's 21st century perspective, those once accepted "rules and roles" of traditional family and church life can now be appreciated and truly valued. However, the flux and flow of change bring us new, relevant psychological insights, as well as spiritual empowerment. We gain encouragement and help in getting beyond the "elephant tracks," and in moving toward holistic renewal and personal transformation. We can now share a more appreciated story of "what the Lord has done for you, and how kind he has been to you." (Mark 5:19).

Chapter 5, looks into the face of those fears and anxieties directly connected with change, and addresses specific personal, developmental challenges. Learning to decode our discontents, understanding the deeper message of our fears and anxieties, turning our discomforts into opportunities can take the sting out of change. Although "the perennial necessity of change is not going to change," the Spirit of Truth will guide us into everything that is true. (John 16:13).

Chapter 6, accesses the psychological and spiritual blessings of change. Since we cannot give what we do not have, it is essential that we look deeply into our minds and hearts, as we renew our commitment to live a meaningful, productive life. One of the key considerations in this chapter is the understanding and practice of spiritual discernment. Its significance for personal and relational integrity, and the steps that lead to decisions about change are examined carefully in the light of the gospel reminder that new wine must go into new wineskins. (Mark 2:22).

Chapter 7, presents a "how to" finale. After scrutinizing the issue of holistic change from several different perspectives, the bottom-line concern for personal and spiritual renewal takes us to practical ways of empowerment. Fortified with helpful insights and amazing grace, we go toe-to-toe with the demands of change. We see clearly: spiritual practice is not a "new age" trend. It is about appreciating our unique value. It is about our witness to God's presence within, and beyond us. It is about being the salt of the earth, and living at peace with each other (Mark 9:50) every day in every way. Meditation, wordless prayer, and holy presence are among the ingredients of our personal and spiritual renewal. This book is an invitation to understand, accept, and resolve the wounds of change, and to move resolutely forward toward holistic transformation.

1.

UNDERSTAND THE SIGNIFICANCE OF CHANGE

"You must change your mind and heart and believe the good news." (Mark 1:15)

The Meaning and Value of Change.

Change by any other name will still be a formidable challenge. For most of us mortals, experiences of change feel more unsettling than their accepted definitions might suggest. To become different, altered, modified or transformed, whether for good or ill, can be downright frightening. Change may indeed signal both danger and opportunity, but the possibility of peril usually gets top billing. Staying stuck in a bad situation has little to commend it, yet opportunities for a life-enhancing change rarely, if ever, include assurances that comfort is right around the corner. Change is not for the feint-hearted. It calls for courage, for determination, for keen awareness, and for God's amazing grace.

Arm-chair philosophers assure us that "shift happens," that shift means change, and that change shares meaning with variation, fluctuation, improvement, or even decline. But however it is defined, change is about movement. Greek mythology seems to have caught a basic idea about the value of change in its story of Proteus, the god of change. According to a famous tale, Proteus had the habit of stretching out on the large smooth rocks along the Aegean shore. There he enjoyed his daily bask in the high noon sun. That is, until his arch enemy saw a chance to do him in. When soft snores sounded the "ok" of Proteus' siesta, the enemy sneaked up, and entrapped the sleeping god in a large, heavy fishing net. When Proteus realized what had happened, he simply changed himself into a little spider, crawled through the net, and took refuge under one of the rocks.

Today, we still remember Proteus. Those tiny, amoeboid creatures whom we first met in an introductory biology class, were named protozoans because like Proteus, the god of change, they too could easily change their shape. Stories of ancient gods make fascinating, imaginative tales. But we mortals do not have the capacity for boundless and easy changes. We are not endowed with Proteus' signature quality: easy change-ability. For us any kind of change is a real challenge, an option that is hardly ever easy. Living with change is a very personal, womb-to-tomb experience. From our earliest moments of life, we become the person we are because change happens. From day one, on through adulthood, into old age, human building blocks called cells are about their business of changing organic chemicals into the live entity called "me." This dynamic process includes the building-up and breaking-down, the birthing and dying of who we are. This integrated connection between living and dying, between stability and change seems somewhat paradoxical. Biologists use the word "homeostasis" to signify the necessary balance between the body's need for both chemical stability and developmental change, for both sameness and newness.

From a psychological standpoint, any change process involves not only a willingness to learn something new, but also the willingness to unlearn what is already deeply embedded into one's personality. For this learning and unlearning process to take place, motivation for change is essential. And this work of motivation involves developing attitudes, values, and habits that support change, in spite of the initial feelings of pain and discomfort. Insofar as change is a cognitive process, new information and learning techniques may set the stage, but emotional prompting and support are also essential. Yet even when information and support are readily available, the actual willingness and determination to change is not yet "in the bag." Becoming a change-able person requires that we be willing to take in, absorb, and assimilate new information, new perspectives, and that we then reflect prayerfully on the change we need, and on the grace we ask.

Just as in other losses, so in our dealings with change, our first healing task has us coming full-face with its necessity, its reality. We must also acknowledge and work through the pain, otherwise it will manifest itself through some symptoms of abhorrent behavior, or even physical dysfunctions. We work against ourselves by not adjusting to the new demands of change, by ignoring the important healing tasks that require us to reinvest our emotional and spiritual energy in personal growth, in positive attitudes. I have also found that a brief consideration of our habits of thinking can help us recognize a few cognitive disorders, ones that might impede our personal and spiritual growth progress.

Am I susceptible to exaggerated impressions that give me a skewed picture of reality? Do I see events from a personalized, egocentric perspective, one that places me at the center of attention? Do I evaluate a particular situation from only one favored perspective? Am I in the habit of thinking in absolute terms of good versus bad, of either—or, rather than allowing a more inclusive narrative? Do I hold to the primitive thinking style of allowing very few options, instead of the more advanced cognitive style that welcomes many options in the spirit of creative change?

The Danger of Sameness.

Most of us know from our own experience that we seem to have a built-in tendency for "digging in" and defending against any kind of change. The temptation to remain fixated at any point in our mental and spiritual development is so great that pathologies of body, mind, and spirit often result. To a large extent, full-scale well-being depends on how we come to understand, accept, and resolve the many different forms of change that we encounter. Remaining locked-in to limiting or narrow perspectives cuts down on our ability to live fully, to commit whole-heartedly to health of body, mind, and spirit.

We may look with fascination—and perhaps with some envy—at how easily the lizard-like chameleon can protect itself by readily changing its colors. Mimicking its surroundings, and evading its predators gives this little aficionado of change a head start in its survival efforts. Survival for our human species, also requires change. But in our case, conscious awareness, and deliberate choices add to the complexity of who we are, and who we are becoming. Not only in our surviving, but also in our thriving, we find ourselves in the on-going flux and flow of life. Even death itself has been described as another transformative experience, another needed change.

When we are faced with the "hot button" issues of separation, transition, and renewal, how effectively do we meet these challenges for change? Do we simply react in the lower-brain's stimulus-reflex mode? Or are we aware of our spontaneous attitudes, of our need to become more mindful and skillful in the way we adapt to nature's necessary changes, to God's transformational invitation? Because change is a universal life-engendering phenomenon which touches every aspect of our personal identity, it makes good sense that we make every effort to understand and embrace the challenge of change.

Focusing on the discomforts of change is easy. What about the discomforts, or even dangers, of sameness? How maddening life would be without change. In *Out of the Flames*, Lawrence Goldstone and Nancy Goldstone, the authors, take us back in time to the Middle Ages when creative thinkers were burned at the stake for daring to "think outside the box." In both theology and science, the accepted rule was "the old way is the only way." Change was simply not acceptable. Favorite family photos do a good job of capturing sameness, of freezing a moment of time. There I was, only ten months from God. Our family album shows me being held by my Dad. If sameness were Nature's rule, I would not be here, now many decades later with change written all over me. Except for (or perhaps including) genetic predisposition, and the essence of eternal being, not much is the same. The years have been witness to countless physical, mental, and spiritual changes. With all its successes and failures, hopes and disappointments, joys and pains, dangers and opportunities, the advantages of change win by a large margin. How hellish life would be if sameness had its way. Fortunately, the glory of God, and Life itself is thumbs up for change. (Psalm 33:5)

Change as an Attachment Challenge.

Our human need for attachment is Nature's gift, a way of helping us to survive. Back through the corridors of time, a primitive cave environment made close attachments absolutely essential. Even today, babies and young children require warm, loving attachment to a primary caregiver. For human development to move forward on a trajectory of healthful growth, attachment must be more than just physical. In *The Developing Mind*, Daniel Siegel shares his work on the neurobiology of interpersonal experience. He underscores the importance of the affective connections between right brain intuition signals of caregiver with the baby's initial right brain developmental needs. Siegel states that "Attachment research suggests a direction for how relationships can foster healthy brain function and growth: through contingent, collaborative communication that involves sensitivity to signals . . . and the non-verbal attunement of states of mind."

When good-enough parenting has allowed for healthy attunement, secure attachments during childhood and adulthood can be established. This means an increase in positive emotional response to any life situation, and a decrease in negative relational attitudes. In effect, early secure attachment experiences will automatically reduce the natural discomfort that any life-change brings.

When it comes to attachment problems related to change through separation, Mari is a good example of an attachment-separation challenge. As a young three year old child, she remembers vividly the stressful atmosphere in her home. Being especially sensitive to the relational tensions between her parents, she readily developed nervous tics, upset stomach, and exaggerated fears. Perhaps because she was never physically abused, it took Mari many years before she made the connection between her parents' emotional turmoil and their inconsistent attunement with her. Fortunately for her, she was able—with psychotherapeutic help—to get beyond her early attachment problems, to deal more effectively with later-life challenges of change.

As part of her healing process, Mari had to face honestly the negative elements of her early formative years. She had to acknowledge the truth of her attachment deprivations, to clarify in her own mind and heart, her parents' good intentions but limited capabilities. She had to review her painful experiences of separation which clearly reflected the glaring inadequacies of her early attachments. In sharing her developmental narrative, Mari recalled how traumatic her graduation from grade school was. With academic honors, and various achievement awards to her credit, she delighted in joining her classmates for the celebration. The honored young graduates all enjoyed the evening together with their family and friends. But when it was over, Mari realized that she would never see her friends again, because unlike them, she would be going away to a private high school. She did not meet the challenge of this necessary separation very well. That night Mari cried herself to sleep. Even now, in her advanced adult years, she can easily recall the sting of that early adolescent separation.

In his classic study, *Separation*, John Bowlby reminds us that our early attachment and separation experiences have significant effect on our later life expectations. If, for whatever reason, our safety needs were not sufficiently satisfied by good-enough parenting, then we will continue to experience painful feelings of vulnerability and want—exacerbated by any kinds of life change. It has been suggested that even a traumatic birthing experience may intensify a person's sensitivity to separation anxiety. From a personal perspective, I believe there is much truth to this suggestion. Both my Mother and the nurse who attended her at my birth assured me that mine was a very difficult and traumatic birthing experience. After these many years, separations of any kind, especially from those I dearly love, continue to cause me much discomfort. Life changes of the attachment-separation kind, even of the apparently benign forms, all leave their particular wounds. They leave unique challenges for personal healing, for enhanced holistic well-being.

Healing Moments

1. Sit comfortably, upright, relaxed.
2. Breathe deeply and slowly for several seconds.
3. Remember a warm attachment experience to a trusted loved-one.
4. Change unsatisfied attachment needs by loving, comforting your "inward child."
5. Know that you are a word spoken by God, who does not speak nonsense.

6. Trust that with all your faults and failures, God loves you unconditionally.
7. Sit in the silence, and love God who lives in you.

Unresolved attachment issues may cause significant problems, may add unnecessary discomfort at any point along life's path. Back in 1890, William James wrote that a great source of terror for infants is being left alone. Today when we reflect on this concept, we can readily connect the "dots" about fears of aloneness. Very often, this fear of the solitude needed for personal and spiritual growth is rooted in very early fears of separation and abandonment. Returning to Bowlby's research, he warns us not to minimize the "experiences of separation from attachment figures, whether of short or long duration, and experiences of loss or of being threatened with separation or abandonment." These experiences block the smooth course of development and exaggerate one's sensitivity to the fears and anxieties of separation. As we learn to better understand our formative experiences, to more clearly appreciate the long-term effects of separation, we can more effectively meet the challenges to our thinking and feeling about the many forms of change, and how they affect our holistic development.

For those of us committed to the integrated way of life, a holistic perspective is essential. This focus includes at least a casual acquaintance with our human brain, and how it can help to explain our thoughtless, even hurtful behaviors. When we trip ourselves up with our refusals to change, or our refusals to "think outside the box," our psychological and spiritual well-being is at risk. When we allow long-time friendships to disintegrate because of a primitive-brain response to a "theological detail" then a long, hard look at such behavior is necessary. The primitive brain operates, for the most part, without feedback from the control center located in the frontal lobes. Without the higher responses of our thinking brain, Godly virtues of any kind are down-the-tubes.

Our primitive—sometimes referred to as reptilian—brain is a fight-or-flight reflex action that has its advantages when immediate danger threatens. It is a health hazard if it operates at random, and a spiritual danger when it prevents higher-order insights and compassion. Learning to evaluate or accept change when primitive brain wiring is operational, results in a lose-lose situation. Although we cannot "unwire" our primitive reflexes, we can learn to become aware of our thoughtless reactions, and to hold them in "neutral gear." Ken is becoming more aware of his spontaneous critical reaction when more liberal Christian perspectives on family planning conflict with his more conservative views. He is learning to hold his beliefs more gently, to categorize opposing views as creative rather than loathsome, and to feel more comfortable with the resulting ambiguities. To put his attitudinal change another way, Ken's advanced control center is out-voting his primitive brain.

The Now of Change.

Awareness as an educational skill helps us understand the foundational concepts related to our acceptance of change. However, it is the quality of our spiritual life that helps us deal with the deep pain and suffering that come with change. Whether the wounds and pain of change diminish or enhance our life experience is up to us. Spirituality supports our choice for fullness of life. Sara comes to mind when thoughts of painful change and spiritual support converge. When I first met her, she was a resident in a nursing home, and at age 86, had dementia, along with a very bad habit of spitting. The nurse who asked me to "do something for her" reminded me to keep a safe distance from her bed, where she preferred to spend most of her time. At our first meeting, Sara met my self-introduction as expected, with a hearty spit in my direction. I knew very little, almost nothing, about her. Yet her behavior suggested to me that somewhere under her dementia was a truck-load of pain. Conversation was out of the question, so I pulled up a chair to a safe distance, spoke slowly, and softly to her about nothing in particular, and spaced my comments in long silences. When I said quietly, "see you tomorrow, Sara," she gave me another big spit. This routine went on for several visits. Then, about the seventh visit, she did not greet me with a spit, and as I took my leave at the end of my visit, Sara said clearly, "come back?"

Although my encounter with Sara took place decades ago, I remember her situation very clearly for several reasons. She was "disabled," angry, unsociable, and ornery. I was a young pastoral counselor, not sure about the best way to comfort her. The shepherd David and his meager resources came to my mind. But in my case, my "weapons" were: a compassionate heart, a soft and sensitive voice, and a vibrant spiritual life. While I sat quietly most of the time, saying nothing, simply being in God's presence, amazing grace did its mysterious, healing work. Sara's fear of change, probably exacerbated by her move to a strange environment, became neutralized by the hidden Spirit within each of us.

Like Sara, we all face life-changes. Some of them are heartbreaking: loss of independence, change in living environment, separation from those we love, feelings of spiritual abandonment, and the list goes on. How do we accept these challenges, and at the same time deepen our relationship with God? No easy answers come to mind. However, a dynamic facet of change, one of those "in process" aspects that makes change so unpopular might point us in the right direction: ambiguity. Ambiguity has been described as "the flow of change," as the moving point, the uncertainty of change. Perhaps it is here that we best learn to accept the challenge of change.

Not the primitive, but the advanced brain lives comfortably with ambiguity. Elkhonon Goldberg tells us, in his informative book, *The Executive Brain*, that the frontal lobes of our advanced brain are uniquely human, that they have a critical role in the success or failure of our human quests. He points out that this "leadership" part of our brain is connected to our intentionality, purposefulness, and complex decision making. This part of our brain is like a conductor-to-orchestra, a general-to-army, or a chief executive officer-to-corporation. Any damage to our frontal lobes results in poor—even dangerous—judgments. In our relationship with Self, God, and Other, prefrontal cortex plays a central role. In forming our goals, objectives, plans of strategy and action, and in evaluating our intentions and actions, the "executive brain" takes over. Or at least it should! If the primitive brain moves in under these circumstances with its fight-or-flight reflexes, our relationships are headed for disaster. Goldberg's information assures us that we "must have the flexibility to adapt different perspectives on the same situation at different times. Dealing with inherent ambiguity is among the foremost functions of the frontal lobes." The primitive brain cannot do this. It cannot see things in a new light, creatively. Rather, it operates in easy absolutes. "Stiffness of mind" could indicate the sluggishness of the frontal lobes through early on-set of dementia. Or perhaps it results from a simple case of laziness, of unused capabilities, of refusal to accept the gospel's challenge of change.

Even though we would rather not deal with the ambiguous aspects of change, we must. As fully functioning human beings, we are commissioned by Providence to meet a multitude of change challenges, and to help others do the same. One of my favorite Easter stories is Luke 24: 13-47. Here we find two travellers walking to Emmaus, deep in conversation, caught in the ambiguities of the recent changes that had shattered their hopes and expectations. While they were absorbed in serious discussion (frontal lobe activity) the Divine Presence was with them, unrecognized. The "Stranger" who joined them heard their concerns and complaints, and offered no easy answers. Instead, he plied them with questions, and eventually explained to them the scriptures. As always, Jesus was not intrusive. He waited, and then accepted their invitation to "stay with us." Shortly after, the travellers recognized Jesus in the breaking of bread. Here, the ambiguities, and uncertainties of change were recognized, understood, and accepted. These folks on the way to Emmaus had mental flexibility, came to see the recent happenings in a new light, and opened their minds and hearts to the great "change according to God." Their good example is with us still.

Besides the troublesome ambiguity of change, another aspect of this challenge toward personal and spiritual renewal deserves some attention: the "happening now" of change. We will consider again in the pages ahead, the practice of mindfulness, of living in the present moment. However, a brief reference to the now of change might be helpful in this initial overview. As sincere pilgrims on our way to God, we already know that we carry many wounds of change. We are also aware that in recognizing, naming, and accepting these vulnerabilities, we open ourselves to communal support, and consequent empowerment. But are we sufficiently aware that this renewal happens in the now-of-time, or as Tillich wrote, in "the eternal now."

When it comes to the now of change, we are well-advised to be cautious, to be ready for the humbling task of acknowledging the many ways we avoid change, now. The most difficult challenge involves opening ourselves, directly and immediately to the change that is happening now, right at this present moment. Why fret about the "what ifs," or "might have beens?" Meeting the needs of today's change challenges requires our attention, time, and energy. Read into Jesus' message what is there: the troubles (changes) of today are challenge enough. Undue concern about yesterday's or tomorrow's problems scatters my focus, dissipates my energy, and accomplishes nothing. The now of change does not discount the learning value of assessing past attitudes and behaviors. Nor does it dismiss lightly, strategic planning for the future, all immensely valuable frontal cortex accomplishment! The now of change simply follows Jesus' teaching about not having undue concern about how we look, what we accomplish, the mistakes and poor judgments we have made. Now is what it is, an eternal present.

Getting bent out of shape about egoistic neglectfulness of the past, getting too absorbed in hopes of the future may have minimal benefits. But living in the what-is-happening-now of change holds the healing power, the personal comfort of God's amazing grace. Again, this does not mean we ignore the wisdom of former insights. Nor does living in the now mean avoiding to plan prudently for necessity. Living in the now puts emphasis on accepting the challenge of change in this present moment.

Healing Moments

1. Stop whatever you are thinking about for a few seconds.
2. Breathe deeply and slowly for several seconds.
3. Zero-in on a particular concern that keeps invading your mind.
4. Place yourself in God's Presence, and unconditional love, right now.
5. Picture your concern being stuffed into a big UPS carton.
6. Hand the boxed concern over to the Higher Power.
7. Take another deep breath, and deliberately hold a full smile. Now!

Spirituality and Change.

When we consider the deep personal change that comes with holistic spiritual development, we are reminded of Karen Armstrong's inclusive study of the Axial Age. In *The Great Transformation*, she tracks the evolving change through history toward human solidarity and compassionate concern, both for ourselves and for everyone else. In that long ago era of great change, there was Jesus, our Model, calling us even as he does today, to leave the hind-brain ways of "an eye for an eye and a tooth for a tooth." (Matthew 5:39-40). He in effect calls us to love our enemies, pray for those who act hatefully, be compassionate in all our interactions. (Matthew 5:43-48). This call to change is not less essential because of the passing years. Rather, it is becoming increasingly important for individual, communal, and global survival. And beginning at the personal point of practice, this transformative change is our life's challenge.

In *Science and the Modern World*, Alfred North Whitehead assures us that even in theology we can find gradual development, change in search of truth. He points out that the famous John Cardinal Newman wrote eloquently of the developmental changes in doctrine, that all through his life he continually supported this perspective. But what if our different views clash? Whitehead assures us that this is not a disaster. On the contrary, it is an opportunity. "In the evolution of real knowledge these challenges of change signal potential blessings."

Yes, even in our concerns about the inward, spiritual development of life, change has an important part to play. Recent research polls suggest that the majority of those randomly questioned identified themselves as believers in God, as interested in living a meaningful life, i.e., one that encompasses all aspects of human experience: physical, intellectual, and spiritual. Settling for anything less can diminish life's possibilities. But settling for more brings us face-to-face with the challenges of change. In the Christian context, Mark 1:15, shows Jesus inviting us to a fully engaged here-and-now life style: "You must change your minds and hearts and believe the good news." These Scriptural words have inspired any number of commentaries that have focused on the necessity of heart and mind change. However, in our acceptance of this change challenge, we are often brought up short by our own question: "How?"

In revisiting mediaeval history, we find that theology and spirituality together formed a single discipline. As time and circumstances changed, so did the understanding and practice of these human ways of keeping connected with a higher Reality. During the Middle Ages much of the "civilized" world felt the seismic political-social-religious changes that tore families and nations apart. The great Reformation and its Counter Reformation left many "absolutes" in the dust. Yet change would have its way. And today in our 21st century, we still live with the remnants of those huge paradigmatic shifts.

The Enlightenment years brought still more change. This time the pendulum swung in favor of those scientific endeavors which flaunted concrete evidence. The inward life of the Spirit took back seat to experimental data, and a new set of "absolutes" took over. But this too changed. Today we have little or no patience with misconstrued ideas or vague abstractions about spirituality. Today, legitimate science no longer connects the inner quest for God with an abnormal or pathological repudiation of the physical. Now spirituality stands solidly against outdated, erroneous ideas.

As a pioneer in the serious study of spirituality, William James focused on the unique inward experiences of adult persons. According to his psychological investigations, he found that wholehearted belief in a higher power Who cares for us unconditionally, results in physical, mental, and spiritual well-being. For James, spirituality (religious experience) has little room for abstract ideas of God, Who is intimately connected to our everyday experiences—including our challenges of change and renewal. In arguing for the existence of God, James shows how it is possible that human consciousness may survive death, even though it depends on the physical brain circuitry during ordinary life. Beyond finite consciousness, but continuous with it, unconsciousness serves as a source of moral and physical energy which feeds our hunger for spirituality, our desire for God. This is an interesting and challenging thought. It suggests that with this felt empowerment, we humans are better able to grapple with, and get beyond life's many diverse changes. The understanding and practice of spirituality can turn us loose to create and enjoy the challenges of this life, now, even as we anticipate a Reality beyond. In both its universality and its particularity, the practice of spirituality inspires us to meet the challenges of change, to live in creative renewal, and to embrace life fully.

Gaining familiarity with life's spiritual dimension involves an understanding of the human capability for both cognitive and intuitive insights. In his *Pensees,* Pascal gives clear evidence of his conviction that spirituality is a way of living, a way that involves every aspect of a person: body, mind, and spirit. He argues convincingly that to focus primarily on "reasoned" data alone, to divorce intellect from feelings keeps us locked in a closed and narrow world. To deny, distort, or destroy the person's unity of mind and emotion, to compromise the integrity of body, mind, and spirit, is to deny, distort, or destroy the holistic experience of spirituality. This in turn can compromise the human capacity for living productively, for meeting the challenge of Jesus' call for change.

In trying to clarify the importance of the inward, spiritual life, it might be helpful to emphasize its distinguishing relational quality. Spirituality is most certainly about relationships, those with ourselves, with others, with our environment, and most emphatically about our unique experience of God. Of course skeptics run about, mocking the very idea of a Life Force, and denying the existence of God. But reputable and sober data suggest otherwise. The mocking and denial of Reality hold as much verity as a blind person denying the beauty of Picasso's art, or with as much validity as a deaf person denying the harmonies of Mozart's musical genius.

Many centuries ago, the Christian Church Father, Gregory of Nyssa held that in spite of our human limitations, the renewing qualities of inward reflection, of spiritual practice opens the way for a deeper, empowering relationship not only with God, but with self and others. Although it promises relational advantages, the practice of spirituality is not without its reasonable demands. At the top of the demand list, spirituality calls for our on-going holistic development. This includes our inward renewal.

Unlike the crustacean lobsters, crabs, and other carapace creatures who periodically shed their exoskeletons, then grow a new carapace to accommodate their increase in size, we humans are not so emphatically reminded to do away with cramping habits, ill-formed concepts, or dysfunctional relationships. Or are we? Surely migraine headaches, irritable bowel syndrome, situational depression, lower back pain, high blood pressure, and other human discomforts give ample signals that something is wrong, that something must change, that developmentally we might be stuck. In our trying to get unstuck, it can be helpful to give up the fantasy that life is supposed to be a no-change experience.

Like many adolescents, I too was dragged kicking and screaming out of my favored fantasies, especially those taken-for-granted religious and spiritual absolutes. Growing up Catholic in the '50s assured comfort and security to all who kept the "rules." And if I slipped up? There was Confession, the priest's absolution, and a few Hail Marys. It all seemed so simple, so safe, so certain. It was only later, as a maturing adult, that change shattered my complacency, that it tore apart my egocentricity. Deep inward spiritual change can carry terrors akin to the fear and anxiety felt during a natural disaster. In my early adult years, I found it a fearful revelation that the good life requires an authentic spirituality, a way of life that includes every aspect of who I am, what I think, how I feel. It even requires that I listen deeply when intuition "speaks." What a wake-up call! What a mandate to change! Spirituality if it is worthy of its name, remains open to change, to inclusive attitudes, to creative approaches to life. It discourages uninformed acceptance of the status quo.

Change comes, ready or not! No one is spared the challenge. We all experience its stings and stabs. One way to meet these challenges for renewal is by opening ourselves to a personal spiritual aggiornamento. This essential renewal process can get started with a few basic reflections. First, befriend yourself. With all your incompleteness, you are a word, a name spoken by God. As Thomas Merton reminds us, "God does not speak nonsense." Second, captain the course of your own growth and development. In freedom and prudence choose values and actions that allow for your creative change, for your physical, mental, and spiritual advancement. Third, accept Pascal's wager: Believe in God's unconditional love, and live accordingly.

There are many good definitions of spirituality. My own home-grown definition, based largely on personal experience finds it best described as "a way of life." Talk comes easily, but living the change required for a viable spirituality is far from easy. My early commitment to living the spiritual life took me behind convent walls where I delighted in prayer, meditation, and daily communal rituals of worship. Every day the daily routine helped keep each aspiring novice focused on the inward life. As a very young nineteen year old adult, the semi-cloistered life seemed to me to be a kind of spiritual luxury. But it only "seemed to be." I had yet a lot to learn about changing my mind and heart, and living the good news of Jesus' invitation. It took years of prayer and practice before the inner truth of being in God slowly took root within me. As Tillich put it in his *Morality and Beyond*, the will of God is not a strange law, an external demand of obedience. Rather, it is the "silent voice" deep within us that calls for change of mind and heart. This "spiritual presence" enables us to remain flexible, to respond appropriately in the immediate, concrete situation. It keeps us grounded in the higher Reality while, at the same time, guiding us through the labyrinthian paths of cultural confusions. Indeed, without the practice of authentic spirituality, external command to be good can backfire and drive us in the opposite direction, toward the evils of self-centeredness.

One of the most freeing, exhilarating, empowering experiences of my spiritual journey came with the profound, yet simple realization that every individual person is called to live a close, intimate, and loving relationship with God. It does not matter much, how, where, or what we do. What does matter is our "being," our willingness to follow Jesus' mandate: Change and believe! Our being (in the Spirit) is foundational to the choices that change requires of us. One of the most respected spiritual directors, Carolyn Gratton, tells us that "Truly life-giving decisions and actions are born, not from raw vital-functional ability, but from reflective hearts that are connected to the deepest, most energizing sources of life." Complete openness to the inspiration and empowerment of the Holy Spirit is called for. This openness to the Holy Spirit implies an openness to the challenge of change. We need this openness, this flexibility because we may not yet be, in fact, the person we are called to be by God. This big change within us can begin to happen when we learn to be silent and receptive to the Invisible Divine Presence.

But what about fruitfulness, productivity, and good works? Unless these outer activities are rooted in our inward, spiritual life, there is the real danger that our investment in these good works will keep us from sincerely giving ourselves to God. As Merton reminds us, "God does not need our sacrifices; He asks for ourselves." In the final analysis, God wants our change of mind and heart, our holistic integrative development. God wants our transformation in Christ. This transformation will not lock us into an abstract "inner life" that neglects or avoids the beauty and sensuality of the material world. Instead we will experience greater appreciation and respect for all facets of life, within and far beyond our global world.

Our way of approaching the process of change, our way of living the spiritual life involves how we imagine and understand Divine Reality. When our image of God is primarily that of a demanding, controlling judge who expects perfection, we can hardly escape the conviction of shame and guilt. What human among us could possibly live up to standards of "perfection?" If this is the unfortunate case, then as Anne E. Patrick tells us in her *Liberating Conscience,* "Our moral energies will be spent on efforts to keep secure by keeping the rules, with the result that our fundamental trust is placed in the rules and in those who sit and interpret the rules in our Christian communities. We will feel betrayed if the rules change, for they have been the focus of our life decisions." On the other hand, when we believe God's creative and compassionate love is unconditionally ours, change holds no real threat. God can ask new things of us; God can "change the rules," and still we trust.

Spirituality as an integral part of our holistic development has its ordinary advancement requirements. And these "ordinary virtues" directly or indirectly affect our change-ability. They can be expressed in the "language of spirituality" and are worth our serious reflection:

1. <u>Accountability.</u> Regardless of our "belief system" we bear the consequences of our thoughts, words, and deeds. A person's willingness to take responsible action, and at the same time to remain open to change, to growth, allows spiritual development to move forward.
2. <u>Dialogue.</u> Meaningful verbal exchange, whether it be with ourselves, with others, or with God, deepens and builds productive relationships that support us in times of change. However, deep listening remains the cornerstone of good dialogue, and a key factor in discerning God's ways.
3. <u>Respect.</u> Commitment to thoughtful and sensitive interactions with self and others is fundamental for our inward growth. The understanding,

acceptance, and genuine esteem for ourselves empowers us to meet challenges of change whenever they face us in the routine happenings of our lives.
4. <u>Courage.</u> The ability to face the uncertainties of on-going, everyday circumstances calls for personal determination and fearlessness. This quality of mind and spirit enables one to face all sorts of difficulties, while remaining firm in conviction, yet open to the new possibilities of change.
5. <u>Diligence.</u> Holistic spiritual development requires our constant and earnest effort to remain both firm and flexible. Because no set-in-stone method for holistic growth can be universally prescribed, each person must ask, search, knock, and persevere along the path that best supports one's growth and change in the way of God's truth.
6. <u>Awareness.</u> Being cognizant of the present moment and its connection to a broader spectrum of Divine Reality may be considered the sine qua non of personal and spiritual maturity. The antithesis of keen consciousness breeds a kind of psychospiritual myopia that disallows the possibility of holy discernment, enlightenment, and creative change.
7. <u>Compassion.</u> Having concern and sympathy for the feelings and experiences of another does not sufficiently identify the depth and breadth of com-passion, i.e., the strong feelings with and for another. This pathos, this loving identification with oneself and with another, opens us to amazing grace, and to the mind and heart change that Jesus calls for.

When we mindfully do what needs to be done in the here-and-now of our lives, when we develop habits of expectation, and acceptance of those opportunities that change can bring, when we live even the ordinary virtues as best we can, then we become firmly rooted in life. Karl Rahner, one of the most respected theologians of our time, has predicted, "The Christian of the future will be a mystic or he/she will not exist at all." By "mystic" Rahner meant a person with a genuine experience of God in ordinary life. And in her essay on "All Things Are Changing," Joan Chittister reminds us that ordinary life is filled with demands for change, that not even the spiritual life is changeless. She writes that nothing requires more trust on our part than the willingness to be open to the unknown, so that God can fill up in us what is needed, so that creative change can happen, so that we can be transformed in the likeness of Christ. Our Christian mission, then, is to become whole persons, to share with others the blessings and challenges of creative change, to make the good news live, now!

Reflective Moments.

1. To what extent have you understood and accepted the significance of any kind of change in your life? Why is change so often a problem? What is your usual response to change?
2. In what ways might your early life experiences of change have influenced your present attitudes and reactions toward any challenges of change, transition, or loss?
3. What attachment and separation difficulties might be impeding your efforts to meet the challenges of change as you move forward in your life?
4. How are you attempting to meet the everyday challenges of your life, and in what ways have these attempts been successful—or unsuccessful?
5. What practical advantages can a holistic perspective of your development offer in helping you address the personal and spiritual challenges of change in your life?
6. In its most essential meaning, what does the spiritual dimension of life mean to you? How does it relate to a holistic view of human existence?

2.

KNOW THE MANY FACES
OF CHANGE

"Go home in peace, and be free from your trouble." (Mark 5:34)

Change in Its Different Forms

Change has many faces. Like the Greek theatre masks, some of these faces project the illusion of gladness, others of sadness. On the stage of real life, the many different kinds of change are not always—if ever—so clear-cut. At first, change may be completely unwelcome. Later it may seem like a blessing. The way that any experience of change affects us depends to a great extent on our own sensitivity, on surrounding circumstances, on personal attitudes.

Jan was eight years old when she, her parents, and younger brother had to make many moves because of her Dad's World War II work for the U.S. government. Jan took these family moves as part of "the war effort," their contribution toward victory. She adjusted well to living six months here, and twelve months there. In adulthood, she had no problem moving periodically when her professional work required it. Her childhood friend, Beth, was a different story. Beth lived all her formative years on her family's comfortable estate. Parents (and grandparents) and two younger siblings felt "safe and secure" in their privileged home life. For Beth, moving across country for her college years was almost a traumatic experience. Two different, unique persons with two different, unique experiences of change!

Common reactions to discussions about change include: "Let's not talk about that!" "It's too depressing!" A reflex reaction against any talk about change is really an effort to avoid talk about loss, or even death. Yes, death is a definitive loss, an absolute change. But, believe it or not, it is not necessarily the most difficult change to resolve. The four-letter word that is a conversation stopper is "loss." Common experience supports the fact that we prefer to steer clear of any talk about separation or loss. Unless we are forced by circumstances to include loss experiences in our therapeutic narrative, we avoid the topic, and refuse to mention even the word. Although it is a shared human experience, loss is labeled as negative, morbid, depressing language, as inappropriate for friendly round-table discussion. The result? Few of us are adequately informed about the nature of loss, and the change challenges it always drops at our feet.

Although there are many different kinds of change, focusing on just a few general categories helps us to identify the more familiar ones. The loss of material objects, or familiar surroundings can involve a major life-change. Depending on circumstances like foreclosure, or fire losses, not much imagination is needed for empathic understanding of such abrupt change. To say that losing a treasured object, irrespective of its monetary value, is "only a material loss" may invite an immediate response: mud-in-the-eye, or worse! Thoughtless comments about cherished lost objects deserve a put-down.

On a hot, humid Saturday evening in July, Hank and Jen decided to cool down at their local movie theatre. While they were absorbed in a favorite Hitchcock adventure, three adolescents roamed through their neighborhood until they found an open window on the second floor of Hank's and Jen's quiet house. After the movie and an iced-coffee refresher, they returned home to tribulation. Jen's treasured memento, a signet ring of her Dad's, given to her Mom as a pre-engagement gift many decades ago, was gone. For her, this ring loss was a painful disconnect from her parents. It opened again the wounds of change that their deaths had caused.

Then there is relational loss. This type of change can be especially complicated, depending on the kind and quality of the personal connection. My earliest observation of a heart-breaking loss takes me back to the summer of my senior year in high school. As a very conscientious "candy-striper" nurse's aide at the local hospital, I saw many life-changes: some for better, some for worse.

As I recall, the afternoon rain did little to relieve the steamy feel of that long-ago August heat wave. In those pre-central-air-conditioning days, the loud buzzing of a few floor fans stirred the stagnant air, but gave little relief. At this worst possible time, a new elderly patient was wheeled onto our floor. She was dying an excruciatingly painful death from terminal colon cancer. The stench of decay enveloped everything within and around her. Her relentless heart-wrenching screams sounded down the long corridor, through the closed doors, and beyond. Never before (or since) have I been exposed to such horrible extremes of human pain and suffering. To my astonishment, the nursing staff went about their routine duties, apparently without concern for the dying woman. With signs of emotional upset on my face and in my voice, I asked the Charge Nurse why this patient was not being given pain-relief medication. "It is not yet time for her next injection." This response baffled my common sense. However, medical protocol in the '50s still followed unchanged medical rules; consequently, administration of morphine shots in non-military hospitals was rigidly and tightly controlled. Developmentally, this event bolted me out of any adolescent idealism I may have still harbored about authoritarian rules, and unchanging absolutes. Fortunately, death brought this poor woman peace. Fortunately too, the relational rules between patient need and medical allowance have also changed. Today pain relief is given as needed.

A few days after this incident, I was helping the nurses in the Pediatric Unit. There I met diminutive five-year-old Harry, a gentle little fellow who spent almost as much time in hospital as he did at home. When little Harry was ready to be wheeled up to OR for his scheduled procedure, he turned to me, and pleaded, "Miss Anne, please come with me?" I leaned over and whispered, "Stan will be with you in OR, and I'll wait here 'til you come back." He smiled weakly as Stan wheeled him to OR. I wondered if, in his childlike simplicity, he might have known that his life would probably end before it had really begun. Here was a different kind of relational change for Harry and his parents. This was loss of possibilities that might never unfold.

That same afternoon, Marie was admitted to the women's ward. At age twenty-two, she was only five years older than I was. Her diagnosis: uterine cancer. Her prognosis: terminal. In helping the nurse make Marie as comfortable as possible, I noticed her ashen complexion, tired expression, yet graciously appreciative attitude. Until Marie crossed my path, the finality of change-by-death was, in my mind, primarily an old folks happening. She had been married approximately a year when her condition was diagnosed. I left her bedside, nursing my own sad heart, and had no words of comfort for her young grieving husband waiting in the hall, trying to blot dry his spastic rush of tears. This felt like another painful relational loss: dreams ended, hopes eroded, change definitive.

Toward the end of that same summer, a high school senior had been admitted to one of the semi-private rooms. Fred was my own age, in the final stages of a losing battle with leukemia. My being at Fred's bedside, just long enough to replace a pitcher of ice-water was an experience in deep sadness. Attempts at friendly chat met his silence and forced smile. My heart ached for this young guy who would never have a chance to reach adulthood. At the end of my work day, on my way home, I visited the hospital chapel. No prayers, just numbness marked my presence. Truly, I felt stunned. The unknown old woman, little Harry, gentle Marie, unsmiling Fred: What do these definitive relational changes mean?

Every kind of change leaves its wounds. In addition to material, and relational losses, we can experience inter-psychic loss, an inward experience of "what might have been." Functional loss involves change in our accustomed place in a family or social network. This particular kind of change is familiar to retirees, especially when their identity was largely connected with their work roles. There is also systemic loss. This change can challenge us at any time. We all belong to an interactional system. These might be clubs or other organizations, or even more loosely held social connections. When they change, we need to acknowledge our losses; we need to attend to our wounds.

Aging with Grace

Ageing is yet another kind of familiar change, one that is especially persistent, and unnecessarily painful because of our present-day cultural norms. Unlike some Eastern cultures where the aged are revered, our Western norms show little appreciation for the inner wisdom, and valuable life experiences of our elder folks. However, with the increase in senior population, septuagenarians and late-elders are making their own significant contribution to the understanding and acceptance of change, transition, and loss.

When she reached her early nineties, Elisa began in earnest to distribute her "stuff" to nieces and nephews. (She had no children of her own.) Having always been an active member of her Church community, she enjoyed the benefits of those sincere friends who helped her make "final arrangements." Along with her living will, her Church community advised her on other matters of personal concern. Having lived through the Great Depression, and several global wars, Elisa was no stranger to the pain of loss, or the challenges of change. She knew first-hand its many faces and forms. She can easily recall the mixed joy and pain of her engagement celebration in 1943. In the midst of the laughter and congratulations came the sadness of unexpected change: Her husband-to-be received notice that he was to report immediately for military assignment. Her response? She wiped her tears, and within a few days, joined the supportive services here on the home front. Her motives? "Do what you have to do!" "Move with the tides and turns of life!" "God's ways are beyond my understanding."

But how did Elisa manage to keep a focused mind, and a happy heart through so many ups and downs of her ninety-plus years? This is not an easily answered question. Probably Elisa herself would be unable to fully explain her positive attitude. Yet, her story tells an inspiring tale of true simplicity, of genuine trust. She knew how to be comfortably alone with herself, and with God. Although she never wrote her life's story, she passed on, through her verbal sharing, the good times and the hard times of a second generation immigrant family. She found fulfillment as the "matriarch" of her extended family, and as an active member of her Church. She also delighted in serving her community in hidden ways. Elisa's narrative would hardly make the New York Times Book Review — or any review for that matter. She is one of those "little people" that Jesus loved so dearly. She knew how to open her mind and heart to God's touch, how to get beyond the troubles of change. And how to live her elder years in peace and joy!

The ageing changes and loss experiences of Ida take a very different trajectory. Unlike Elisa, this octogenarian is dealing with crippling arthritic pain, and periodic asthmatic attacks. She has carried a very painful change-wound deep in her body, mind, and spirit for almost two decades. When I first met Ida, she was marking the anniversary of her husband's death. Like Elisa she was a devoted member of her Church community. But in Ida's case, she hesitated to seek comfort and support from her many friends. The reason? She acquiesced to her husband's wishes, and helped him end his life. At face value, this seems like a horrific action. But when she asked herself, "Is it right to do good, to relieve pain?" the shadow side of her decision took on a new light.

Approximately ten years before he died, Ida's husband began experiencing very unusual persistent neurological symptoms: severe clinical depression, recurring hallucinations, anxieties, and terrifying panic attacks. At the time of his treatment little was understood about his condition. Various pharmacological attempts to control his symptoms were not effective; in fact, the intensity of his extreme pain was increasingly unsustainable. Together Ida and her husband prayed for spiritual discernment. After years of suffering, he could no longer endure the torments that were ruining both his and Ida's lives. Trusting in God's mercy, he took an over-dose of meds, and slipped quietly into the night. Ida had carried the burden of her complicated loss for too long. Resolution was necessary, but it would not be easy.

Sometimes the usual mourning rituals may not be enough, and the survivor is left without any sense of support and healing. In Ida's case, a compassionate review of her loss narrative could set the stage for understanding, for accepting this complex loss and grief situation. Within the family, within the Church community, a climate of trust, of tolerance, of tender, compassionate response helped Ida to eventually open herself to God's healing power. When certain feelings or thoughts are not allowed to be explicitly shared because of loyalties or taboos, they might surface as particular mental or physical symptoms. As Walsh and McGoldrick point out in *Living Beyond Loss,* "When communication is blocked, the unspeakable is more likely to be expressed in dysfunctional symptoms or destructive behavior." They go on to include certain factors that complicate the loss experience, such as, suicide, secrecy, myths, shame, guilt. Some individuals seem to take their loss challenges in stride, and deal with them without too much difficulty. Others can feel greatly uncertain in their attempt to accept death as part of life, as an opportunity for transformative experience.

For Ida it was her Church community that eventually helped her to accept the fullness of God's love, and the practical, compassionate support of others. They helped her to see the up-side of loss: a chance to develop a clearer sense of her priorities, a greater capacity for empathy, a sense of her own courage and capabilities. Ida was fortunate to be an integral part of a living Faith community that embraced her as she faced the consequences of a terrible death loss — one that threatened to swallow her in a black hole of despair.

Like every other life stage, elder-life holds its own kind of change challenges. In order to avoid being a burden to their children, an increasing number of senior adults are choosing to opt for continued care retirement living. The advantages of this decision would easily fill an average-size notebook, with security issues leading the long list of incentives. This retirement move is usually preceded by research analysis, sleepless nights, and prayerful hopes. But for most retirees, concerns about relocation issues, though important, are secondary.

Personal diminishment, like a late afternoon sun, announces the unavoidable fact that night is falling, sleep is near. Ailments of every sort can be identified: crippling arthritis, assorted pains and aches, periodic "senior moments"—all unwelcome life-changes. Ask Marita, a recent retiree. She will fill you in about routine therapies, appointments with gerontologists, and other medical specialists that absorb big chunks of time and energy. This is all part of the ageing scene no matter where one chooses to live. Change is everywhere! However, according to Marita, the mutual support of retirement community friends and neighbors forms a treasure beyond price.

According to the available statistics, residents in continuing care retirement communities enjoy a fruitful, extended life-span. From my own studies and observations, a vibrant spirituality is also a key factor in longevity. Reported findings in a relatively new discipline called neurotheology, offer concrete proofs that the serious pursuit of prayer, meditation, and compassionate caring does have a positive impact on holistic well-being.

Not simply during our later years, but at every age we are faced with the challenges of change. Do you remember those gawky pre-pubescent "ageing" symptoms of the ten-year old? Lips and nose seemed disproportionately noticeable on a once familiar face, while feet found new ways of tripping over themselves. Then came the more serious changes of adolescence: body parts with a mind of their own, stubborn skin eruptions, emotional ups and downs, and other assorted annoyances. Early and middle adulthood brought its own change-challenges: on-the-job adjustments, marriage and family responsibilities, and much more. Yes, life is a never ending growth process that continues onward until we near the threshold of death and new life.

Healing Moments

1. Sit up straight and comfortably in a chair, or on a pillow.
2. Take several slow, deep breaths; ask for inward guidance and discernment.
3. Recall to memory a brief line from your favorite hymn, or prayerful reading.
4. Softly and slowly sing or say your chosen words over, and over again.
5. While singing or saying your thoughts, be grateful for your voice, memory, thoughts.
6. Continue this private "meditation" for several minutes.
7. As the day's happenings allow, continue to "sing" in your heart, and thoughts.

Death and Dignity

The Death of Ivan Ilych by Leo Tolstoy tells how in spite of his pain and fears, Ivan was able to die with full acceptance. Before death moved in closely, "He wept on account of his helplessness, his terrible loneliness, the cruelty of man, the cruelty of God, and the absence of God." Ivan asks of God, "Why hast Thou done all this? Why hast Thou brought me here? Why dost Thou torment me so terribly?" A few hours before death arrived, and after an extended and terrible struggle, Ivan's negativity, anger, and fear dropped away. He had finally given in to God's way. In place of darkness, there was light, there was joy. As he drew his last breath, death was no more! Here was a man, an ordinary good man, whose focus in life had been fenced-in by his ambitions, and control needs. When he no longer denied his finitude, God's love broke through his protective boundaries. His limitations were acknowledged; he opened himself to Life.

Returning again to our Model, Jesus, and his attitude toward death, we find him giving no indication that death is a big problem. For Jesus, being open to God in the present moment was the key to eternal blessing. Similarly for us, being open to the empowerment of the now-moment assures our personal and spiritual ability to face the loss and change challenges waiting for us along life's path. Many were the miles Jesus walked from the villages of Galilee to the crowded streets of Jerusalem. All through his public ministry, Jesus lived with full awareness of his life's purpose. When his brutal execution took place, he died, not necessarily without screams of agony, but certainly with great dignity and courage. Incidentally, dignity here is defined as an inward quality, not an outward appearance.

While he lived, Jesus never hesitated to heal the sick, and comfort the dying. When his friend Lazarus died, Jesus wept, and then gave life a second chance. (John 11: 1-44) It is impossible to imagine Jesus doing nothing to ease the pain and suffering of a discomforted person. Wherever he went during his travels, Jesus met the living and dying of small villages, growing towns, and large cities. Hospitals as we know them today, along with their diagnostic machinery were hardly imaginable at the beginning of the Christian era. Consequently, a modern-age image of Jesus keeping anyone prisoner against their will, connected to a steel breathing machine contradicts his dignity and ours.

High technology aside, we can still learn a lot about dying with dignity by listening deeply in mind and heart to Jesus' message. As we open ourselves to the power of his living presence, we learn that dying is not simply an end-of-life happening. It is a dimension of life that effects in one way or another, all our decisions. Consequently, our finite human lives can move toward peace and empowerment by not suppressing the idea of death, but by using it as an incentive to live a Reality-based, transformative, compassionate life.

Death then, brings a change in life, not an extinction of life. In his plea for personal responsibility, for dignified dying, Hans Kung reminds us that in death we do not dissolve into nothingness. "Rather (we) are taken up into that incomprehensible and ineffable last and first reality which is pure spirituality beyond space and time: the eternal, most real reality. There is a transformation through new creation and an eternal hiddenness in God. God is then not only in all things, but all in all. (1Corinthians 15: 28)" Can this perspective on death help us change our negative way of thinking and feeling about our physical demise?

In *Dying With Dignity*, Kung goes on to mention that unless healing (not necessarily curing) is possible, "a fight against death at any price is nonsensical: it is a help which becomes a torment." Genuine healing goes beyond "cure." It offers the needy person, compassionate attention, prayerful listening, and our full presence. Genuine healing of each and any of our wounds, whether physical, psychological, spiritual, or all of the above, takes us yet again to Jesus, our Model, who always opted to take away any kind of suffering. To quote Kung again, "With discipleship of Jesus goes an ethic of responsible shaping of life—from beginning to end." Since God has given us responsibility over the whole range of our personal and spiritual life, then we must stay alert, and always be prepared for the life change called "death."

If as Christians, we are convinced that death is not the final end of everything, then our God-given freedom includes the responsibility to make determinations about our dignified living and dying. An old Latin prayer for the dead says, "Vita mutatur, non tollitur:" Life is transformed, not taken away. Consequently, dying with dignity involves living with dignity now, in this present moment. It means making prayerful choices. It means respecting a key theological principle: "The right to live and the right to die is the nucleus of self-determination." Like Hans Kung, we can rest in Faith that death does not hold the last word, "that I shall be taken up into a last dimension beyond space and time into the eternal life of God; then in the spirit of the Sermon on the Mount, I need not be so terribly anxious about adding a cubit to my span of life." (Matthew 6: 27)

Acknowledging Feelings of Pain

She is unnamed. We know her only as the woman-with-an-issue-of-blood. In Mark 5: 25-34, she is among the crowd following Jesus, but she is not your typical "groupie." According to Jewish tradition, she had three strikes against her: first, she was a woman, evidently alone in public; second, she was considered "unclean" because of her hemorrhage problem. She merited her third strike when she deliberately touched Jesus and made him—and anyone else she may have inadvertently elbowed—"unclean." Driven by her courage and discomfort, by her burning desire to live life fully, she dared to acknowledge the reality of her pain. She braved the crowd; she "touched his clothes." And what did she get for her courage and trust? Physical and spiritual healing: "Daughter, your faith has made you well; go in peace, and be healed of your trouble." (Mark 5:34) Her acknowledgement of her pain led her to a determination that changed her personal pain into fullness of life.

When, like the unknown woman in the gospel, we are ready to acknowledge our need, to admit that, yes, we are ready to accept a change, then healing and renewal can begin. Then we will be ready to examine more closely what the pain of a change loss is really about. Although normal, this kind of change often brings with it feelings of confusion, of emotional upset. This is the challenge of a faithful commitment to personal and spiritual development.

Like the woman in Mark 5: 25-34, we want to be at peace. We want to be healed of our trouble. But we must keep in mind that refusing to acknowledge our pain, blocks our ability to respond appropriately to any kind of change. Like an infection that spreads its poison throughout the body, so unacknowledged pain spreads its refusal of reality throughout our personal experience. We are then held victims of its frightening intensity and surprising complexity.

But the painful feeling is not the end of it. Even our sense of who we are can be attacked and diminished by significant change. The initial shock can sometimes hit like a tsunami. "This can't be happening." "I refuse to believe this loss change." When my Dad died unexpectedly and quickly from a brain tumor, I had great difficulty acknowledging this reality. Alone in my newly furbished kitchen, I screamed out, hysterically kicked cabinets, walls, appliances, and cried until exhaustion took over. Like the waves of birthing pangs, I alternated between painful outbursts, a few moments of calm, and then back to long minutes of "insanity." Without realizing it, I was grieving the loss of my Dad, as well as the loss of a part of myself. I had to fully acknowledge this life-change before I could effectively deal with it.

Because my adult identity was not essentially defined by my relationship with either of my parents, I was not existentially threatened. I experienced painful sorrow, but not anxiety and depression. Yes, I was very attached to my Dad, but I was not defined by my relationship with him. My loss of his physical presence was no profound threat to my own existence. If I had lost a parent while still quite young, my story might have a sadly different twist. But since losses of any kind, and changes of any intensity require a reaffirmation of the self, I to needed to reassess, reaffirm, and support my own identity.

For infants and young children who are helplessly dependent for their survival and well-being on the "mothering" they get from primary caregivers, abrupt loss-changes can be devastating. This abandonment feeling can even linger throughout life, making the possibility of close, healthful relationships problematic. In his study of Charles Darwin, John Bowlby suggests a meaningful connection between Darwin's unresolved early loss of his mother, and his life-long proneness to physical maladies. After his mother's death, the young Darwin was cared for by his older sisters and demanding father, none of whom allowed any mention of the families death loss. Darwin's terrible loneliness was to a significant degree the result of his legitimate needs being totally ignored by those he trusted most. His family's ignorance of his pain and confusion, their inability to comfort and support him, added to the intensity of his pain.

Acknowledging our pain often sets in motion the first step toward resolving life's challenging changes, transitions, and losses. In *All Our Losses, All Our Gains*, Mitchell and Anderson tell us that we cannot get away from the experience of loss, that it is especially painful because "attachment is a human necessity." Even our attachment to places and things lasts through childhood into adulthood. Our appropriate attachments keep us connected to God's creation, to our need to be faithful stewards. The message is clear enough: To be fully human will always involve our being attached, our experiencing changes, transitions, and losses, and our having at times, to feel great pain.

And if we refuse to acknowledge our pain? Then we are left with the residue, the "baggage" that will continue to weigh us down. Small life-changes will seem overwhelming; any losses will feel traumatic. Distress, discomfort, depression will take over. Eventually a heavy price will be paid physically, mentally, and spiritually. Turning away from the truth of what is, the trafficking in unreality, leads to the certainty of increased, unresolved pain.

Experiences of pain, brought on by loss-changes, must be identified, accepted, and worked through. Denying the pain simply makes matters worse. When Louise lost her husband, they were both in their mid-forties. Louise's copious tears were not welcome by her controlling in-laws. They encouraged her to "keep busy," "think of other things." Pastoral counseling helped Louise to see the folly of her family's advice. Once she saw that her painful response to a significant, abrupt change in her life was perfectly normal, she felt free to grieve according to her own needs.

Although there are common factors shared by all grieving persons, the dynamics of pain and neediness remain unique to each individual, to each set of unique circumstances. We all suffer the pain of change in our lives because we are humans living with our natural limitations, with our inescapable finitude. But here is good news: No change in our lives can diminish the presence of a faithful God, or the empowerment of amazing grace. Still we are left with our responsibility to clarify, confront, and accept the pain of our change wounds so they can be eventually healed.

An angry response to any change carries an experience of hurt behind it. When the hurt stings badly enough, anyone or anything can be the target of fury: the walls, the dishes, a loved one, even God. Walls and dishes can be replaced; God is beyond our tantrums, but another person's dignity must be respected. Whether or not the inappropriate, uncontrolled, angry response was deliberately perpetrated, the acting-out person is accountable. Acknowledging pain by indiscriminately exploding in an angry episode does not help the healing process of our change-wounds. In fact, it makes matters worse. Yet anger is a common response to the loss experience and deserves consideration. In most cases, angry feelings do not get out of control. However, when over-reactions occur and show hostility toward others, when feelings of distrust and suspiciousness cause an agitated and severely negative demeanor toward others, then therapeutic attention can be helpful.

Guilt is another response to change, but it shoots its arrows of pain directly at the suffering self. Donna was in her late sixties when she came for counseling. Her husband was becoming more incapacitated as his Parkinson disease progressed. With tears in her eyes, she told of a most recent incident, and her overwhelming feelings of guilt and shame. Her husband sat on the shower stool as she tried to wash his back. Over-tired from her 24/7 caregiving life, she took the washcloth and threw it at him. She was at the breaking point, saw her own need for self-care, and decided to bring her feelings of guilt and shame into therapy. There she acknowledged that the incident of the wash cloth was only the "tip of the iceberg." She had been the over-functioning partner in her marriage for many long years. Her angry explosion left her with guilt feeling about her not being a good Christian, not being able to deal positively with this on-going "nursing assignment, (she was not a nurse), and especially for allowing herself to believe that she must always put the needs of others ahead of her own. Donna confronted her guilt, her concept of a judgmental, punitive God. She also admitted her rigid, primitive moral attitude. When she could finally affirm her value, and open herself to empowering grace, positive change got a toe-hold. However, she still had to confront the residue of a lingering, toxic shame.

Although at the feeling level, guilt and shame seem to be the same thing, they are not. When a person experiences guilty feelings for violating human values and Christian principles, this guilt is good. Balance returns with the acceptance of painful feelings, and regret for inappropriate actions. Shame tells a different story. Shame is personalized, a matter of identity, of a wrong conviction about who I am. Unlike guilt, no lesson can be learned, no growth opportunity can result. Shame can have toxic qualities of self-destruction. A classic example of shame is given in the film version of *Precious*. Here a young woman tells about her experience of traumatic abuse, and toxic shame. She lives with the firm conviction that she is a flawed, useless, worthless "dog." She has been repeatedly raped by brother, by father, and feels totally unlovable. Her thinking, of course, is distorted but no one counters her self-hate. She exists among the throw-away people until a teacher, and a therapist throw her a "life preserver," an opportunity to acknowledge her terrible pain, and to move forward beyond it.

In *Healing the Shame that Binds You*, John Bradshaw points out that toxic shame is basically a spiritual problem. He calls is "spiritual bankruptcy." However, when spirituality becomes a lifestyle, it enables us to experience the fullness of being; it helps us to grow beyond the crippling bonds of toxic shame. Spirituality's trajectory points inwardly to that self-validation and self-empowerment that is sourced in God. This Reality-based lifestyle allows opportunities for personal and spiritual renewal. But can shame ever be non-toxic, or even helpful? Maybe! When it signals our human limitations, when it helps us experience the truth of our finitude, when it clarifies our need for disciplined thinking and behavior, when it energizes our respect for communal relationships, then shame might be helpful. "Good" shame avoids the following destructive "viruses:" perfectionism that insists that you be always right, beyond criticism; blame that requires a victim, a defensive cover-up; muteness that prohibits any attempt at honest self-expression; blindness that refuses to see the intrinsic value of individual persons, and the Great Mystery that enfolds each of us.

Acknowledging our feelings of pain is a first step toward healing our inward change wounds. But it is not the last. Each of us carries within us a universe of creativity, of physiological, psychological, and spiritual possibility, of unending change. And this human condition gives us every reason to "rejoice and be glad." Acknowledging thoughts and feelings of both pain and hope brings to mind Mark's Thursday of Holy Week story (Mark 14: 12-25). In spite of his knowing what was ahead for him, in spite of his knowing that betrayal and suffering were only a matter of hours away, Jesus told his friends to prepare for the Passover feast. How could he converse in loving ways, while knowing the certainty of his cruel murder? Yes, Jesus knew his closest friends very well. He knew that in their weakness they would abandon him during his hours of greatest need. And yet he chose to focus his energies, his full presence on this present celebratory moment. He modeled for us a total trust in his "Abba" and his acute awareness of the "bigger picture." He transcended his traumatic crucifixion, and changed loss into gain. In our own struggles, we must make every honest effort to go and do the same.

Healing Moments

1. Take a brief quiet-break. Breathe deeply, calmly for several seconds.
2. Focus on a challenging interaction with a loved-one, friend, or acquaintance.
3. Recall briefly your feelings and thoughts during that interaction.
4. Acknowledge your responsibility to treat yourself and others with respect.
5. Reflect on the "give and take," on the change challenges regarding your attitude.
6. Trustfully place your change-needs in the hands of God; be open to change.

Dealing Effectively with Change.

"We have met the enemy, and he is us," so spoke the famous Pogo of comic strip fame. Change, transition, and loss happen. No amount of moaning and groaning can possibly expunge from life, these challenging happenings. But as Pogo reminds us, we are the "enemy" in so far as we refuse to meet the challenge of what is!

We might ask ourselves how we will meet the demise of a close relationship, or of the end of a long-time marriage. Bob and Amy met in college and married immediately after graduation. Neither of them had grown yet to the point of personal autonomy, self-confidence, or interdependence. When Amy realized that she was "out-growing" her partner, she worked at encouraging

Bob to acknowledge their "misfit." Although frightened by the probable outcome, Amy met her challenge full-face. A few years of professional help made the relational issues clear. In this case, the ending was a positive, mutual agreement. Amy and Bob ended their marriage, found compatible partners, and have remained good friends to each other. They were both able to understand and resolve their need for a significant life change.

The loss of meaningful work, because of job loss, or retirement presents another real challenge. In some cases this life-change also challenges financial security, or the family lifestyle. Physical deformities resulting from war, accident, or congenital problems bring their own kind of change-loss. Unacknowledged though they are, we need to meet the challenge of every kind of loss, including that of our pets. Circumstances that negate our personal or professional dreams can also cause great distress. In any and all of these life-change situations the bottom line reads: Effectively meet the challenge.

Since this is not an "easy answers" book there are no lists to follow, or "things to do" which might offer immediate relief from the painful wounds that follow in the wake of any kind of change. Instead we turn to a few realistic, effective ways of meeting the challenges as best we can. This brings us back to Pogo, and to us. Instead of looking outward, beyond ourselves for the causes and remedies, we are well-advised to look inward, to get to know, accept, and appreciate how we can be integrally involved in meeting the challenges we face.

Change in any of its forms can shake and shatter the comfort of the status quo. Change can push us toward the legitimate, life-enhancing desideratae of life. Though often hidden somewhere within the mystery of ordinary circumstances, all our change challenges carry their veiled treasures of wisdom, grace, and healing. When significant changes disrupt our comfortable routines, we have work to do. Like any good detective, we want to know what is going on, especially within ourselves, to make us feel so uncomfortable. If we look deeply enough, we will find that the clues for our healing are "not in the stars" but within our own minds and hearts. It is within ourselves that the healing wisdom and power can be found. There is no "silver bullet," no easy rescue plan.

When Jesus experienced change at his baptism in the Jordan River, he chose to spend some time in the silence and solitude of the desert. There in the stark, barren wilderness, he showed us by his example, how to meet the challenges that change brings. He allowed time and space for quiet reflection; so might we. He spoke to God; so might we. He made difficult decisions; so might we.

In chapter 10 of Mark's gospel, a rich young man—evidently quite contented with his privileged way of life—approached Jesus with a worthy question. Perhaps this well-to-do somebody felt a passing desire for something more meaningful in his life, something more than material affluence, or social influence. But when Jesus' invitation implied the need for a values, and lifestyle change, the rich young man walked away. He chose not to meet the challenge of growth; he chose to avoid change—even a beneficial change.

In order to distract ourselves from the wounds of change, we often fill our lives with things-to-do, places-to-go, people-to-see. Yet a nebulous feeling of emptiness keeps us unsettled. Can we face the discontents, pain, and confusion of unrelenting challenges of change? And beyond this, can we take a long, hard look at our personal capabilities and limitations? Can we effectively meet these challenges of growth and change?

In his study of the psychological and spiritual needs of the growing person, James Fowler points out several developmental levels that mark our passage from early to advanced personhood. His scholarly study, *Stages of Faith* focuses on the psychology of human development and the quest for meaning that can help us track our own psychospiritual needs as they relate to change. We begin our inward development via a gradually evolving self-awareness. As we move into our pre-puberty years, literal interpretations of a belief narrative help give meaning to our experiences. In adolescence, religious beliefs give us comfort as a self-identity begins to emerge. But a mature spirituality, a developing inner life has us facing tensions of individuality versus conformity. At this point we must begin to accept personal responsibility for our beliefs, values, and attitudes relating to the inevitable change challenges that confront us.

Whether at age four, or forty, (or far beyond and in between) every person has known the complex good-and-bad entanglement with some form of change. Human consciousness takes this cognitive, affective awareness to its highest potential. Biology, psychology, sociology, anthropology, spirituality, and related studies continue to expand our knowledge of who we are. The relatively new field of neuroscience offers a long list of published research findings on human consciousness. Distinguished scholars like Damasio, LeDoux, Greenberg, Siegel, and Newberg (to mention only a few), are giving us a deeper appreciation for the holistic function of our body, mind, and spirit. With this more inclusive perspective about ourselves, our chances of effectively meeting the changes that challenge us are greatly increased.

And why is this enhanced perspective so significant? Unhealed wounds of change can interfere with our experience of a peaceful, productive mind and heart. Unhealed wounds of change interfere with our ability to "Go home in peace, and be free from your trouble." (Mark 5:34) In helping to free us from our troubles, myths and symbols are worthy of respectful attention. We know that the postmodern digital age is here to stay. But let us not minimize the ageless value of meaningful myths. In formal dictionary terms, a myth is defined as a story that carries a belief. However, this description hardly discloses the significance and value of a story about reality that embodies a sacred happening. Truth has often revealed itself in the form of myth. Along with our paradigmatic myths, our personal and spiritual growth and renewal can also be advanced through symbols. In *The Sacred and the Profane,* Mircea Iliade mentions that symbols help us find a way out of a particular situation, help us open ourselves to the larger Reality. "Symbols awaken individual experience and transmute it into a spiritual act, into metaphysical comprehension of the world."

When rightly used, myths and symbols help us share spiritual experiences which are beyond theoretical speculation. They help us access the spiritual life, life beyond pure rationality, beyond those abstractions devoid of real life. When rightly used, both myths and symbols invite us to open ourselves to new possibilities for intuitive, and effective ways of dealing with our change challenges.

As a symbol of living Faith, I chose the turtle for its enduring, steady presence. Turtles were at home on planet earth long before Abraham and Sarah made their earthly appearance. Native American spirituality has long honored the turtle as "keeper of the faith." Its enduring presence, its record of survival through countless eons gives ample reason for honoring the turtle with such favored recognition. As an undergraduate biology major, I spent long hours of laboratory time learning about, and then dissecting a turtle. While I found these prehistoric creatures deserving of great credit for their tenacity and survival skills, I found them graceless in movement (except in water). Nor did they have the attractive coloring of birds and butterflies, or the majestic aura of the great eagle. So why did I, in late mid-life, choose the turtle as my symbol, as my reminder to be faithful to the spiritual life, as my reminder to keep moving forward in spite of change?

Quietly enduring, gently present, slowly determined, without flashy fan-fare, these characteristic qualities seemed enough reason to admire the turtle's approach to life. Besides, they fit my own general preferences and inherited temperament. Even today, a life-size plastic turtle sits comfortably on my car's dash board, reminding me to "take your time," "Be attentive," "Live in God's present moment." Having spent the early years of my childhood enjoying the woods, creeks, meadows, and farmlands of rural Bucks County, I fell easily into my Dad's love for Nature and its non-human creatures. Cats, dogs, horses, even little grey field mice became "extended family." Snakes, spiders, bees, and worms were not included. But turtles? Back then, they didn't register as particularly interesting, nor fun to have as pets. They just seemed "weird!" Now, however, it is the turtle with its fascinating history, its respected meaning that helps me to stay focused, in spite of "busyness" and the endless challenges of change. This humble symbol of enduring, efficient simplicity calls me back repeatedly to awareness of God's empowering presence.

The myth, pregnant with meaning, awaits our discernment, our decision to unfold its deeper message. It seems to me, that Charles Hartshorne, in his *Omnipotence and Other Theological Mistakes*, takes the bull by the horns, and directly unfolds the deep truth within and beyond several mistaken accounts or "myths" about God. According to Hartshorne's analysis of a few taken-for-granted concepts about God, we humans do great injustice to God. For example, Hartshorne says that omnipotence, as usually conceived, is a false or indeed absurd ideal that in truth limits God, and denies to God any world vibrantly alive. God wants us fully alive, free to make our own decisions. Consequently, a correct spin on the idea of omnipotence is "that it influences all that happens, but determines nothing in its concrete particularity." God's purpose is our happiness, which is God's own happiness, which has no limits. The essential message of an "on track" myth about God seems to emphasize that holistic spirituality is real. God is real, unbounded, unborn, undying, and in this God, "We live and move and have our being."

Like a pointing finger, myths and symbols are meant to help us see beyond their literal meanings to the broader implications of story-told happenings. But we seem to prefer the apparent security of focusing on the "finger," on the concept that can be pinned down, formalized, locked in to serve as an inflexible absolute. We would do better to open ourselves to the "beyond," to God's universal and creative possibilities, to the challenges that change offers us. In the Christian tradition, Jesus gave us no formal, verbal definition of spirituality. Instead, he gave us himself as a living example. By wise inference, we learn from Jesus' example, how to live our Faith here and now: practice, practice, practice! And that practice involves our physicality, as well as our mentality. Every embodied activity or life situation can be a way of experiencing deeper connection with God, with Ultimate Reality. For example, our openness to the many challenges of change can become "the serious business of heaven." This serious business allows the deep joy, the peace, the freedom from trouble that can be ours. (Mark 5:34)

Reflective Moments

1. What are your thoughts, feelings, responses to meaningful, relational changes or losses? How have your responses satisfied your need for healing these change wounds?
2. To what extent and in what ways have you responded to the many challenges that the ageing process brings? How have you avoided the issue of life change?

3. What mourning customs and rituals are you familiar with? In what way have they been helpful in healing your loss wounds?
4. What are your discomforts, hesitations about planning for the end-years of your life? What might help you in this regard?
5. How have you managed to resolve the normal feelings of guilt that often accompany our loss changes?
6. As a spiritual growth reminder, what symbol is meaningful and appropriate for you? In what way does it help you to remember the presence of God?

3.

GET BEYOND THE STRESS OF CHANGE

"And so I tell you, ask and it will be given you; search and you will find; knock and the door will be opened to you." (Luke 11:9)

Stress as an Integral Part of Change

Changes of any kind are never "pure," that is, they are present to us in a complex mixture of positive and negative effects. Stress is one such effect, or more accurately stated, distress is one such effect. In everyday parlance the idea of stress needs no definition. We have no difficulty understanding what stress feels like. When performance pressures escalate, and on-the-job achievement expectations have no ceiling, "that's stress!"

Although stress may have different effects on different individuals, or different effects on the same individual at different times and under different circumstances, its impact is always holistic. Stress always affects every part of who we are: body, mind, and spirit. When stress levels are too high, or too persistent, burnout can result. The entire person experiences physical pain, mental malaise, and spiritual disconnection.

As an ER nursing supervisor, Lori's successful career at an inner-city teaching hospital was turned on its head when her husband was diagnosed with an inoperable brain tumor. Her two young adult children refused to accept their father's demise; her husband wanted her near him, day and night. Her determination to meet the needs of family and patients was heroic, but her capacity for enduring the long, stressful days was limited. Soon migraine headaches warned of immanent physical, mental breakdown. Like any normal human person under similar circumstances, Lori had to face reality. She had to choose between letting stress do its dirty work, or allowing change to give its realistic options.

Decades ago, Hans Selye gave us the results of his extensive and in-depth study of stress. Selye's work back in the 1950s identified stress as a response (not a cause) of the pressure we feel. He preferred the word stressor to describe any outside cause for our discomfort. So exactly what is stress? According to Selye, "Stress is the nonspecific response of an organism to any pressure or demand." He goes further to distinguish two different kinds of stress: eustress and distress. When we celebrate a happy occasion, the planning and preparation may increase the intensity of our responses to related activities. But this is eustress, or good stress. It is the distress of negative pressure and demands that plays havoc with our holistic experience. Certainly Lori had too much concentrated distress in her life. She experienced negative stress (distress) from "outside" circumstances, but she also experienced "inside" distress from her own inner attitudes toward what she perceived as her responsibilities.

For Lori, as for any of us, the inability to meet the demands of any kind of stressful circumstances can deplete our immunological resources. This leaves us vulnerable to any assaults made against our good health. Lori's close friend, Pam, found herself in what felt like a no-win situation when her mother had major surgery, her daughter ran into academic problems at college, and her just deceased uncle's estate needed her legal expertise. Pam had difficulty coping with these family issues while keeping up with her busy law practice. Within six to ten months, she was being treated for colon cancer. According to her physician's opinion, Pam's particular type of cancer was probably "caused by stress." In non-medical language, Pam's immune system was shot-to-bits; she had no defense against invading pathogens, even the ordinary genre that challenge us on a routine basis.

According to Selye, in most instances, problems with disease are rooted in our inability to adapt to the stress, along with the virulence of the invading germ. Selye goes on to prove that the whole person undergoes a complete physiological response as it tries to adapt to the demands of stress. He calls this holistic response the General Adaptation Syndrome. Since life is what it is, we cannot avoid feeling some degree of stress. The trick seems to be in how we meet the outward and inward stressors. Or, to put it another way, beware of over-taxing the adaptation response which, if unchecked, can result in death.

Except in cases of extreme distress, how we handle the ordinary stressors we meet can depend on our psychological perceptions. If we are unaware of our neurotic tendency to always meet the needs of others, we may one day find that the ability to adapt to on-going stressful demands is "broken." Leanne is a good example of perceptual "blindness" that could be disastrous. For years she had always been there for her family, friends, and acquaintances. No matter the inconvenience to her personally, she supported and cared for others. According to her thinking, "Why shouldn't I help others? This is the heart of my Christian commitment." Leanne never questioned, or evaluated the stress that she felt, or the increasing discomfort that snuck around the fringes of her mind. Why should she complain? She had so much to be grateful for! Then one evening after teaching her late class at the city's community college, she had a surprising experience. As she stood alone on the platform, waiting for her train, she had an overwhelming impulse to jump onto the tracks. As the idea to jump exploded in her brain, and the compulsion to self-destruct gained power, Leanne ran to the nearest bench, and held on to the seat with white-knuckled intensity. Within minutes, calmness returned. She arrived home safely. The following day, she consulted with a counselor-colleague, and began work on her hidden stress issues.

The human body, mind, and spirit has its own wisdom, its own ways of knowing, warning, coping, resolving stress challenges. Each of us as unique persons must identify our own particular ways for discerning how much stress we can take without endangering our well-being. Fortunately for Leanne, she became aware of the changes in her behavior. She met the challenges of her neurotic tendencies and the stresses they caused.

In order to meet life's adaptive needs, an inventory of available resources can be beneficial. But no matter how we perceive and understand these resources, our individual sensitivities remain major factors. Consequently, using psychosocial research data can help us identify to what extent we are "inhibited" or "uninhibited." For uninhibited babies, loud noises have an energizing effect, but for inhibited infants loud noises cause distressful cries. So our spontaneous responses to environmental changes are directly connected to our inborn "wiring," to our unique predispositions. An understanding of such basic factors as biochemical physiology can better help us to change the way we relate to stressful circumstances, and consequently to enhance our well-being.

We know from our own experiences that how we perceive a situation can be directly related to the level of stress we feel. Perceptual clarity can befriend us by making us more mindful of the stressors which may be within us as personal limitations, or may be outside us as environmental factors. Feeling stressed may be unpleasant or quite painful. But in any case, it rings a warning signal: all is not well! On the other hand, perceptual opacity may at first lessen our awareness, keep discomfort at arm's length for a while, but eventually the price of ignorance, of avoidance must be paid. When stress gives us signals indicating that change is necessary, our conscious (and unconscious) perceptions can help forward the work of controlling stress and encouraging change.

Broadening and deepening our perceptual capabilities equips us to meet more effectually everyday challenges of any kind or duration. This concept might well serve as one of our stress-control mantras. But there are also those small-print words of warning that we ignore at our peril. They wisely remind us that we must not overlook the lethal damage that negative attitudes, disparaging thoughts about self and others can cause—even when they are well below the level of consciousness. Self-ignorance acts as a serious handicap when it comes to acknowledging, understanding, and responding appropriately to the stress of our life-changes. We may not be able to control the crises of change that disrupt our life's journey, but we can follow Victor Frankl's advice, and control our attitude toward self and others. We can be aware of the way we perceive and respond to change.

Developing healthful attitudes reminds us again to stay open to, and accepting of the challenges of change. Healthful attitudes generate positive experiences, not distressful ones. Since change is an intrinsic part of our personal and spiritual well-being, we need not be hesitant in opening ourselves to its challenges. It is probably safe to say that everybody loves children—except perhaps those personalities like W.C.Fields! Using the symbol of a healthy child, we can gain broadened perspectives by visiting our own "inward child," that part of us that is positive and affirming, that represents our enduring essence. When we listen closely to our inner child, we learn many things, especially about trust, solitude, and love. Paul Tillich tells us that justice and power are integral to love. Our inner child, while not disputing this, will focus on love that also encompasses trust and solitude. The affectionate trust of our inner child asks us how genuine, real, extensive is our trust of self, and of God? Trust can sustain mistakes without shame. It can believe in truth when change signals a challenge. Child-like trust accepts the reasonable demands of responsibility, but it refuses the neurotic dictates of perfectionism. Our inner child knows how to be comfortable in solitude where creative dreaming and "scheming" empowers the growing process. Our inner child knows the lightness, the therapeutic value of spontaneous laughter. From our inner child, we can learn much about the freedom of God, about how we can unreservedly choose to be the person God wants us to be. This inward freedom keeps the stressors we encounter, and the stresses we feel, well below the point of discomfort or danger.

Healing Moments

1. Sit quietly. Breathe deeply for several seconds. Close your eyes.
2. Feel your arms, legs, and entire body relax.

3. Speak silently, lovingly to yourself. Remind yourself that in spite of your human flaws and limitations, you are a treasured part of God's Universe.
4. You have a right and responsibility to say "No" or "I prefer" when you discern that a request is intrusive or too stressful.
5. You can be honest with yourself. Your happiness is your own "job description." It is not your responsibility to make other "happy campers."
6. In your holistic growth efforts, Jesus reminds you to ask, search, and knock (Luke 11:9), and you will be satisfied. Think deeply about his words.

Spirituality and Stress Control

Luke 11:9 tells us that Jesus said, "And so I tell you ask and it will be given you; search and you will find; knock and the door will be opened to you." For those of us who face the challenges of stressful change, any opportunity for resolution easily holds our attention. When the gospel message advised us to ask, search, knock, we see clearly that stress control must involve our own personal efforts, our own determination to find physical, mental, and spiritual resolution of stress.

Socrates assured us that the unexamined life is not worth living. Jesus reminds us that the examined life requires our questioning, searching, and knocking on the door of possibility. In our determination to meet the many, continuous challenges of stress, are we ready to explore not only our physical, and mental options, but also the way of spirituality, of meditative practice?

The in-depth analysis that Hans Selye gave us about the physiological workings of our human stress-response system leaves no doubt regarding the short and long term effects of hormones and related chemical reactions. At some point in our lives we have heard true stories about a little old granny who had "miraculous" strength when faced with rescuing a screaming toddler who managed to get stuck behind the clothes dryer. The power of human strength and endurance may at times seem to be miraculous, but it is in fact also natural. We are well-endowed to meet occasional fight-or-flight situations. The surge of power that we feel when faced with life-threatening events is Nature's way of helping us survive. But an emergency alert system that operates most of the time can destroy us instead of save us.

Because much of the stress we feel is fueled by our own thoughts of real or imagined danger, we had better know the difference between authentic threats and imaginary ones. Why? If we see everything as danger, the stress of this adaptation effort could be destructive. Just feeling threatened, even without good reason, can trigger our hyper-arousal system, and leave us in a state of compromised health. So what do we do when that fight-or-flight hot button stays on, when blood pressure sores high, when no external release mechanism like running releases the pressure?

True, we may learn favorite coping behaviors. But coping is a short-term strategy, and is ineffectual in the long run. It can also be a slow suicide option. No! Coping will not do! Workaholism, alcoholism, busyness, or any type of addiction does not resolve the stressful challenges of change, transition, or loss. To get beyond coping, to get to practical and immediate resolutions, we need to go inward, to explore the spiritual dimension. Here we learn to connect with the present moment, to become sharply aware of the here-and-now happening. Once we are calm, the insights of a more broad-based perspective can show us creative options for resolution, and can indicate pathways to less stressful experiences.

Being mindful, learning to live in the present moment, is often a challenge. The ability to maintain a relaxed and peaceful presence requires determination, acquired skills, and faithful practice. This approach to stress control may correctly be described as spiritual. The practice of mindfulness, which can trace its origins to any of the world's great religious traditions, may be considered a spiritual practice, but as Huston Smith warns us in his *Why Religion Matters*, the word spirit "has no referent in science's world." Even though our reason goes about its usual work of logical operations when information is available, we can also experience more subtle, even mysterious insights that seem to bubble up from the unconscious. Neuroscientists are coming to recognize that any kind of experience has its origin in intuition as much as—or even more than—it does in cognition. So to include in the approach to stress control, an appreciation of life's spiritual dimension is perfectly acceptable—even necessary.

Considering the cognitive value of mindfulness helps us to perceive more clearly what our stress pain is all about. It "cuts to the chase" and zeros in on our confusion, our embarrassment, our turmoil, our anger, and especially on our neurotic need to have things "my way." Mindfulness helps us to step back and see a bigger picture, to "think outside the box." Mindfulness helps us to be a bit more honest, a bit more compassionate.

Clarissa had a most painful confrontation with her new supervisor, who raised her voice, made false accusations, and threatened dismissal. Clarissa had always maintained a warm but professional relationship with all her academic colleagues. Consequently, she was close to tears at this abrupt and stressful change in her working environment. Clarissa had been committed to her inward spiritual growth for over fifteen years. This included her daily practice of meditation, and mindfulness. When this supervisor became verbally abusive, Clarissa went into her mindfulness mode: slow, deep breathing, out-of-the-box thinking, intuitive awareness. Surprising insights came regarding her supervisor's behavior, including indications of alcoholism, marriage break-up, inadequate skills for her supervisory position. Although she still had to determine what her formal response would be, Clarissa's mindfulness brought the immediate comfort that comes with seeing the bigger picture.

But Clarissa's ability to deal positively with her stressful encounter did not come automatically. She had put a lot of persistent effort into her holistic development, including her daily spiritual practice of mindfulness. Ask Clarissa how she evolved from a very non-assertive person into an appropriately interactive individual and she might say, "I had to get a real sense of myself. This work was a part of my spiritual pilgrimage." Clarissa's personal narrative acknowledges her misconceptions about what it means to live a truly spiritual life. She had to admit that unintentionally, she had allowed distortions to creep into her practice. It was her daily effort given to mindfulness that eventually brought her insight, confidence, and courage.

In his *Spirituality and History*, P. Sheldrake points out that when distortions are "canonized" by ecclesiastical authority over centuries, many people "seriously underestimate important elements of their personal or collective encounters with the Divine." When Clarissa was able to understand and accept her own unique value within the Christian spiritual tradition, she moved toward holistic well-being, which in turn resulted in healthful relational experiences. Among other distorted perceptions, she gave up her childish (not child-like) belief that saints are infallible guides to holiness. Prayer and study led her to realize that over-valued forms of the past can undervalue the gospel message for the present. Jesus himself refused to conform to certain religious ideas of his time. He modeled for us an understanding of wholeness that listens to, and interprets the Message for our own time and circumstances.

When Clarissa became acquainted with James Fowler's *Stages of Faith*, she identified herself as a middle-aged pilgrim, somewhere between Stage Five and Stage Six. She had already critically examined her faith, and had taken responsibility for her conscious choice to live that Faith. She was becoming more open toward differences in the belief systems of others, while staying grounded in her own Faith. She found that her spiritual grounding left her free to better manage her life stressors. She was also wise enough to know that her individual experiences could not be explained adequately by any "stage theory." No one is reducible to stages, even though categorical concepts can be helpful learning tools. For Clarissa her own experience was sufficient enough to encourage her commitment to God, to the meaningful life, to a lifetime of holistic growth.

Happily, Clarissa is now in a "good place" with respect to her holistic growth and development. Stressors continue to challenge her positive inward attitude, but they cannot diminish her comfort level. So, we might ask, what specific tips could she give us for maximizing our own efforts toward holistic growth? Because of her preference for clear, pragmatic directives, she might suggest a few concepts and practices that helped her. From Jacob Needleman's philosophic work, *Why Can't We Be Good?* she might share his wise words: "When the mind and the body receive each other, a new capacity of feeling is liberated, a feeling that sees all things under the idea of Good." He reminded her to search, find, and live her full capacity to love. But her own experience taught her that in order to open herself completely to Love, she had to be able to manage her stress responses.

Clarissa had learned, first hand, that the practice of mindfulness helped her to maintain a more balanced perspective whenever the stressors of change challenged her. Practicing mindfulness had grounded her in calmness and keen awareness. This opened her to new creative ways to resolve the stresses that she faced. To put it another way, her primitive brain no longer dictated reactions to stressful encounters. Mindfulness allowed her to make deliberate cortical responses. She would probably suggest a few of Jon Kabot-Zinn's examples of stress control as given in his book, *Full Catastrophe Living*. His words of honest encouragement include: "As relaxation and peace of mind become more familiar to you through formal meditation practice, it becomes easier to call upon them when you need them. When you are stressed, you can allow yourself to ride the waves of the stress. You will neither have to shut it off nor run away. True, you may be going up and down some, but much less than if you are always at the mercy of your own automatic reactivity." Yes, developing the practice of prayerful mindfulness helps control the stresses of change.

Busyness, an Occupational Hazard

If idleness is the devil's workshop, then busyness might well be its more sinister sweatshop. Why more sinister? Busyness gives the illusion of value, commitment, accomplishment, while too often it signals immaturity, even narcissism. "Look how hard I work!" "See how dedicated I am!" Hard work and dedication are not negative qualities in themselves. However, when we allow them to generate significant, disruptive stress in our lives, we must step back. In Exodus 18: 13-27, we find Moses over-functioning as the leader of his people. When Moses' father-in-law pointed this busyness shortcoming out to him, Moses gave thoughtful reflection to the elder man's observations. Jethro cautioned Moses, "What you are doing is not good," and Moses listened to his father-in-law.

What are we trying to prove by our busyness? That we are valuable, lovable, capable persons? If this is our goal, busyness will never achieve our purpose. In fact, it anesthetizes, blurs, and confuses our clarity of purpose. Busyness' addictive quality overburdens the human body, exacerbates the stress quotient, and in Jethro's words, "is not good." Yes, busyness can become addictive, but before it reaches that point, faulty thinking too often gets it going. How? For starters, busyness keeps us from having the time, energy, or inclination to see a larger, more expansive picture. Perhaps our logic is too tight, narrow, exact, and rigid. We know from experience that a well-lived life requires our flexibility, creativity, openness and trust in that Wisdom beyond human understanding. Busyness keeps us bound to debilitating ignorance. Unfortunately, like all addictive habits busyness does not generate deep, lasting inward peace. The tentative feelings of satisfaction that busyness allows are often counterfeit; they do not lead to our greater personal and spiritual well-being.

When the stressors of modern life wrap their strangling fingers around our best intentions, no one escapes. However, a safe hypothesis might be made about dedicated persons who are at greatest risk for the debilitating busyness syndrome. Beliefs in trite platitudes have convinced too many of us that the more we do, the more acceptable we are. Trudy became a victim of this falsity at an early age. While still a quite young eight-year old, she tried to live her life as she thought Jesus would want her to. As we know, children have not yet had the opportunities to learn, to accept who they are developmentally becoming. Trudy tied her personal value directly to her achievements and to the adulation they won for her. Before long, she had connected the dots between her busyness and achievements to the praise and acceptance she got from her parents, church community, and others. With the onset of adolescence, Trudy's busyness moved out-of-bounds. Finally, in early adulthood, stress took over her life. Confused, exhausted, and dominated by fears and anxieties related to achievement, and "doing good," Trudy was hospitalized for physical and mental rehabilitation.

Trudy's experience could easily serve as an example of how not to be a good person. If access to a wise mentor had been hers, she could have been warned, "What you are doing is not good." Seeing through the superficial accomplishments that seem to bring benefits to family, church, and community, challenges our accepted culture-of-busyness. Physical or mental dysfunction does not enlighten and empower us to get beyond the damaging stress of inordinate busyness. Unfortunately, most of us are not aware enough of the signals we get from our bodies and minds. When we learn to set quietly, to be mindful, we can then begin to read our own stress signals accurately, and to respond more effectively.

Healing Moments

1. Block-out on your evening schedule, approximately 15 or 20 minutes.
2. Take a brief shower, and keep the water at a warm and gentle flow.
3. Using a pleasantly scented gel, gently cover your entire body from head to toe.
4. As you gently massage your skin, be grateful for every part of who you are.
5. Increase the warm water flow, and let the day's stressors be rinsed away.
6. Rest quietly for a few seconds, thanking God for these few healing moments.

Healing the Wounds of Change

No informed person has to be convinced that change was, is, or will be a necessary part of life. At face value, this is easy enough to accept. However, when certain kinds of change cut deeply, their wounds must be examined, and healed. Not unlike the skilled surgeon whose scalpel causes some initial pain in order to effect long-term healing, change very often hurts before it heals.

For convenience, wounds of change may be generally categorized as first, second, or third degree of intensity, with the last being the most troublesome. The least painful, most temporary effects of change may involve feelings of disappointment, annoyance, or minimal discomfort. Here, there is nothing we cannot deal with, nothing that seriously upsets our comfort zone. These wounds of change might include the inconvenience of rescheduling appointments, of having to cancel an evening of entertainment, or of being bed-bound by a twenty-four hour viral infection. We deal with these unwelcome changes without much ado, and then move on with life.

Second degree change wounds are not so easily dismissed. Here we face the kind that cut more deeply into mind, heart, and spirit. Depending on our previous experience, and on our natural ability to handle relational challenges, most adults do fairly well when faced with the more hurtful wounds of a career change, of a friend's death, of a home move, or of similar life changes. But be cautious here! A change in residence, which in itself might seem to be a relatively benign challenge, can be overwhelming for a young widow who must relocate across country, make new friends, and find a teaching job. The challenge of any change wound depends not only—not even primarily—on the kind of change experienced, but more importantly on the "capabilities for survival" of the person wounded.

When we consider third degree change wounds, we are into the jungle of complex, threatening life experiences that defy easy understanding, let alone any facile resolutions. Janis lost her husband after his long fight against cancer. During his last weeks, she was at his bedside, day and night. When Jon died, Janis had her family, friends, neighbors to lend support and encouragement. But three years later she seems worse off than ever. After the funeral, and financial settlements, it was clear that she would have no "money problems." Her health was somewhat compromised because of poor diet, a preference for alcoholic "night caps," and inadequate exercise. In spite of her sister's suggestion that she consider the benefits of talking to a professional counselor, or joining a helpful support group, Janis remains caught in the web of a no-change attitude. Her sister Gwen's gut response may be more accurate than she wants to believe: "Janis, you are committing slow suicide."

In order to heal these wounds that cut so deeply into our identity, into the very depths of who we are, a multi-dimensional strategy needs to be set in motion. This includes relevant data on our personal comfort needs. If because of a privileged life, I am used to having my way, then a hard-hitting, knock-down relational experience can leave me flat-out, with my face in the dust. Depending on how honest I can be, I might focus beyond self onto a bigger picture, then "pick myself up, brush myself off, and start all over again." But what is this catalytic honesty about? Does it hold an insight into how healing our wounds of change might work?

Many years of professional teaching and counseling experience have convinced me that after our most basic needs are met, we must develop a keen awareness of our identity. This involves the determination to understand and heal our wounds of change. Times of change may be the best opportunity to become more sharply aware of our own developmental history, of our habits of spontaneous response to change, of our lingering feelings of turmoil, hurt, anger, or resentment. In moments of stillness, can we muster the courage to be honestly aware of our inner wounds?

Steve was convinced that his wife Lara was a saint. Yet he was having difficulty dealing with her generosity to family, friends, and "causes." He was becoming increasingly concerned about their retirement "nest egg" which was being gradually diminished by Lara's habits of "giving." She continued to satisfy her compulsive habits by using her favorite sayings: "It's more blessed to give than to receive," or "Give and don't count the cost." Because Steve's over-accommodating behavior was a mystery to him, he never addressed his problem. When he finally became aware of what was behind his fear of conflict, beneath his unhealed wounds, he would then be ready to deal better with his "saintly" partner.

In addition to self-awareness, certain basic skills also help to heal our inner wounds. We may not be great interpersonal communicators, but for those of us who know our language well enough, sharing ideas or getting a message across is no "big deal." We manage adequately, sometimes even elegantly. But healing our deep, inward wounds of change requires a less familiar form of communication skills: self-talk.

Child development theorists tell us that young children often comfort themselves when they have had an unpleasant or hurtful interactive experience. They use self-talk. Yes, they actually talk things out with themselves. They instinctively counsel and comfort themselves. A hypothetical example might help. Let's imagine a scenario in which a middle-age woman, Sue, has just returned from an office party. She is not feeling good about a run-in she had with a co-worker. Professionally, she has an excellent record as a certified public accountant. For years she has been in the habit of meditating each morning for at least twenty minutes. Her self-talk on this particular occasion might go something like the following: "It's good that I stood up to Hank with patience and firmness. His sarcastic comments annoyed me, but his negative, almost combative attitude tells me more about his own limitations than it does about mine. I'm far from perfect, but prayer and meditation is keeping me aware of my own intrinsic value and dignity. This is something no one can take from me, something no one else's ignorance can touch. Yes, Hank is not my favorite person. And that's okay! I don't have to like everybody. But I must keep on growing inwardly so that I can heal my own hurts. Keeping a positive attitude toward others like Hank will be a bonus."

Awareness wakes us up to our discomforts. Skills enable inter-relational and intra-relational dialogue to keep us moving in the right direction. But finding the right kind of support can be tricky. Do-gooders are not difficult to find. They pop-up like wild dandelions after a spring rain. Do-gooders mean well, but they are often intrusive, possessive, and downright annoying. They may even be co-dependent: helpers whose whole identity is wrapped up in the person they are "helping." They hang-on like leeches, trying to convince themselves that they are needed. Real, beneficial support comes from those who believe in the midwife approach. These ready-to-help friends encourage and aid according to necessity. They do not invade private space, or out-do their service. Their identity and value as a person is not dependent on being a "helper." They are respectful of everyone's privacy needs—including their own. They are not dominated by the "tyranny of the shoulds." They do not see themselves as being "selfish" when they tend to their own comforts and needs. They are not running away from themselves through their caring for others. Nor are they unduly intent on being seen by others as a "good person." When offered by healthy, compassionate individuals, personal support can go far in helping us heal our wounds of change. And we must take full advantage of every opportunity to increase our inward awareness, to improve our relational skills, and to establish a network of support.

For thorough healing of physical wounds, a good physician will prescribe, along with sterile procedures and appropriate medication, lots of rest, good nutrition, and a positive attitude. In effect, the prescription calls for a holistic (body, mind, spirit) approach. Our inward wounds of change also require an inclusive, systemic approach to healing. When mindfulness generates insights about our hurtful changes, what is revealed in the silence of our keen introspection? Among the uncovered bits of wisdom is a rarely understood aspect of healing: the importance of forgiveness.

Experience has taught me that the concept of forgiveness needs a more inclusive definition, one beyond the usual understanding. Forgiveness involves much more than absolution, excusing, or making allowances. And it carries an overlooked factor: forgive yourself first, so that your forgiveness of others may have real healing power. Sonya had great difficulty pardoning her husband for his many years of abusive behavior towards her. The heavy burden of anger and resentment that she carried wore down her energy, and soured her attitude. She had good reason to be angry—at herself for "patiently" accepting his insufferable actions. And at her husband for his ignorant habits! Forgiveness was not easy in coming for Sonya. The years of abuse had left painful imprints in her mind and heart. Over time, prayer and meditation gradually led her to see the value of forgiveness. Although experiences of abuse are not easily—if ever—forgotten, they can be forgiven. Sonya found that forgiving herself was a first step towards healing. Yes, her shortcomings were real, but no longer reason for guilt or shame. Having accepted herself as part of God's creative love, she was then able to genuinely forgive others. She did, in fact, forgive her husband, leaving his accountability in God's hands. She also made decisions to protect herself from further abuse.

Forgiveness does not automatically wipe-out accountability. When Jim embezzled $50,000.00 from one of his clients, his family lawyer suggested certain protective legal moves that would prevent his family from losing their home and savings. Divorce was one of the results of Jim's criminal behavior. He may have been truly sorry; his wife and children may have whole-heartedly forgiven him. But he was still accountable for his bad behavior. In most cases, we leave the accountability piece to God's "love, power, and justice." We can then rest in peaceful contentment while knowing with Julian of Norwich that "All will be well." However, the accountability factor still holds.

Before my mother's long stay in a Catholic nursing home, I had no personal experience of a significant forgiveness challenge. Small scale forgiveness toward myself and others usually centered around thoughtlessness, even ignorance, but never around a life-or-death magnitude. Within a few months of Mom's residency at the nursing home, abusive administrative policies became evident. Harmful, neglectful modes of management continued to be denied until "accidents" and death brought legal action by the residents' families. Mom's death brought her the fullness of peace, but our family still carries the painful wounds of abuse and harassment. Our sincere and repeated attempts to dialogue with a condescending hierarchical structure were consistently given a deaf ear—even after our respectful, repeated requests for cooperation and compassion. Many months after Mom's death, the spiritual empowerment to forgive criminal behavior finally freed my mind and heart. However, at the human level, accountability needs to keep forgiveness protected from those ill-informed persons who use "forgiveness" as an excuse for laxity, irresponsibility, and selfishness.

Bumper sticker wisdom reminds us that to err is human, to forgive is divine. Without the security and honesty that psychospiritual development engenders, forgiving and being forgiven can too easily be misunderstood. But I have found that right understanding, along with a keen appreciation of the offender's "story" can greatly help to generate a wise compassion. Of course, accountability still stands. Yet, it need not negatively influence the prayerful determination to forgive.

Gifts of Change

Wounds of change, transition, and loss do not usually conjure up thoughts of celebration. Yet, though universally painful, they can be considered opportunities—even gifts—for personal and spiritual advancement. We have already noted that legitimate attachments form part of nature's survival scheme. We have already considered that no change, transition, or loss issue, no matter how benign the circumstances, is without its separation scars, without its need to be identified, called by its right name, and eventually resolved. At our own peril, we ignore, deny, or avoid them. Although much has been published about loss resolution, approaching this life-change issue from a holistic perspective, from the integrated body, mind, and spirit point of view is less common. Consequently, let us look to a classic literary example of what happens when the realities of change, and the pain of loss are not acknowledged, accepted, and resolved.

Henry James gave us his artistically crafted story of change in his famous novella, *Washington Square*. Many years after its publication, the film adaptation was renamed The Heiress. In this film version, we meet Catherine, the exceedingly shy and sensitive daughter of her independently wealthy father, Dr. Sloper, a rather aloof, yet conscientious and successful physician. Whatever losses Dr. Sloper encountered in his personal or professional life, the unresolved loss of his wife when Catherine was born still remains a gaping wound. As she nears womanhood, Catherine's father invites his widowed sister to join his family, to mentor his "backward" and socially inept daughter.

For her part, Catherine tries to assuage her loneliness by deferring in all things to her father's wishes, thereby hoping to gain his love and acceptance. As often happens, the harder she tries, the less she succeeds. Dr. Sloper continues to live with the idealized wife of his imagination, and rarely misses an opportunity to remind his daughter of her gross inadequacies by comparison. However, when Catherine's extended family celebrates her cousin's engagement, Catherine is compelled to join the up-scale social event. Enter Morris Townsend, a bright, handsome, charming young man who must deal with his own kind of loss: his lack of direction in life. Morris easily captivates the guileless Catherine, wastes no time in pursuing the possibility of a permanent relationship with this wealthy young woman, and gets himself invited to dinner with the Slopers.

Morris, wise in the ways of the world, realizes that Dr. Sloper is wary of suitors for his daughter's hand, especially a suitor who has no income, and no work plan. Catherine's naivete', and painful experience of not being able to measure up to her father's expectations add to her vulnerability. She easily capitulates to Morris' charming ways, to his assurances of devoted love. Against her father's insistence that she break with Morris, Catherine goes to the extreme of renouncing her father's wishes, along with her sizeable inheritance. According to their elopement plans, she and Morris are to ride off together at midnight. Midnight comes. No Morris. Hours go by. Catherine agonizes over this latest of her life's many painful rejections until the light of morning convinces her of reality. Until her Aunt unwittingly admonishes her for having told Morris of her determination to renounce her great inheritance, Catherine trusted fully in everything Morris told her.

This stressful change, this crippling loss catapulted Catherine into a different world. She finds her "voice," convicts her father of loveless parenting, and angrily refuses to grant his dying wish for reconciliation. She does, after all legal affairs are settled, become the heiress of her father's great fortune. Seven years pass as Catherine, her Aunt, and Mariah (the devoted house maid) live in the quiet of their comfortable Washington Square home. Periodic visits from her cousin and aunt, and her young niece and nephew, brighten Catherine's reclusive lifestyle. Her days continue to be dominated by a few quiet social events, and many hours at her needlework bench.

On a hot, humid summer evening, after returning from an outing, Catherine's Aunt delivers shocking news: "Morris is in town, wanting to see you, Catherine." After a reflex "No!" she could not resist toying a bit with this mouse-in-a-trap. She invites Morris into her home, listens to his apologies, and attestations of love, agrees to his plan of an elopement that evening, and waits for Morris to return within the hour. Morris arrives promptly, knocks on the locked door, and watches the house lights go dark. He is left pounding furiously on the front door, screaming her name, again and again and again!

This is the traumatic tale of unresolved losses, and the resultant stress that prevents healthful resolution. This is a terrible encounter with life's challenges, one that calls for acceptance of change, forgiveness of self and others, and resolution of hurtful losses. Dr. Sloper had unwittingly destroyed his relationship with the daughter he never took the time to know and accept. The unresolved loss of his wife left him victim to fanciful imaginings that allowed no place for reality, for his daughter. Catherine's discovery of her father's negative feelings toward her brought her hope of parental acceptance crashing down. This most traumatic of human losses remained unresolved, doing its damage, destroying her life year by year.

Without awareness of the systemic damage caused by unresolved loss, without the support of compassionate others, Catherine remains trapped in her ignorance and deprivation. On the other hand, had she been part of a spiritual community, a source of prayerful insights and support, Catherine's story might then have included her decision to forgive herself for her imagined, and real shortcomings. Forgiveness toward her father would have freed her to move forward in her life, to accept her cousin's social invitations, to broaden her narrow mindset, and to engage in personal and spiritual renewal.

The opportunity behind every challenge is often a hidden gift, one that we must allow ourselves to receive. Few would argue against the fact that change often wounds our complacency, threatens our "comfort zone," leaves us in need of healing. Since life is meant to be lived fully, change as an integral part of that living, calls for advancement in our thinking, feeling, attitude, and behavior! For whatever reason, Catherine chose to live in her own narrow world. Paradoxically, her change-free lifestyle carried more long-term pain than change-ability would have caused in short-term discomfort. If Catherine had been part of a compassionate, caring community, her chances for better understanding and accepting her own limitations and capabilities could have been greatly increased.

It is worth repeating that loss changes of any kind require reaffirmation of self. Catherine's unhealthful attachment to her father, then to Morris, left her feeling empty and vulnerable when they were gone. However, the "gift" of her loss enabled Catherine to take a woman's stand against her father's neglect. Eventually she stood up to Morris. These are no small accomplishments. Had Catherine given more time and effort to asking, searching, and knocking (Luke 11:9), to developing the spiritual dimension of her life, she could have opened herself more readily to the gift of change. Her life could have been happily transformed.

Reflective Moments

1. What significant stressors have you encountered recently? What was your immediate response to these stressors?
2. In what way can stress be defined as change? What kinds of cognitive, affective, and spiritual effects does stress usually have on you?
3. In what specific ways does your spiritual life/practice help you keep a balanced kind of busyness in your life? How does your busyness become unbalanced?
4. Many individuals are unaware of the driving force behind their over-accommodating behavior. How comfortable or uncomfortable are you when refusing a request? Why?
5. Co-dependency has been called the kind person's occupational hazard. What do you understand by co-dependency? How might your spiritual values help you avoid this hazard?
6. In facing the issue of forgiveness, what do you find is the most difficult part of this healing practice? Why? How can your spiritual discernment help you?
7. To what extent are you aware of the systemic damage caused by unresolved losses that can accumulate over time, and cause serious damage to body, mind, and spirit? What significant change challenges might you need to examine, and resolve?

4.

APPRECIATE THE RELATIONAL NATURE OF CHANGE

"Go home to your own people and tell them what the Lord has done for you, and how kind he has been to you." (Mark 5: 19)

Treasured Remembrances of Solidarity

The work of healing our wounds of change calls for a good grounding in self-appreciation. This in turn calls for a family voyage, a journey back into the relational history that helped to form and nurture our personhood. If we take this visitation seriously, we can expect surprises, challenges, laughs, and even valuable insights. Getting reacquainted with our relatives opens the "doors of perception" on our family members, and especially on ourselves.

The grown-up generation of both our immediate and extended families gave us their time, affection, and those hand-me-down stories of long ago happenings that even in our mature years we still treasure. Grandmother's sea voyage from "the old country" to the new, Uncle John's hitch-hiking adventure from east coast to west coast may not be true in every detail, but when told by a master-teller, we are awed. But more than their well told tales, the presence of their caring love, and the lived values they handed on to us, stay with us, nourishing our minds and hearts, and giving us hope.

If we were lucky enough to have a few "characters" in our immediate family, we should consider ourselves especially blessed. Voyaging back in memory helps to clarify a legacy of challenge, change, and renewal that affirms the marvel of who we are. On this kind of voyage there are no hideaways. Every family has its secrets and legends, its saints and sinners, its own litany of unique characters. In one form or another, many families have an Aunt

Maggie who fingered her prayer beads faithfully every day, praying for her loved ones, as she sat alone in the silence of her little apartment. We might have an Uncle Joe who never frequented a church. Why should he? According to him, he and God never had a quarrel! We might have a great-grandmother Tess who walked two miles in freezing weather, through drifts of snow so she could get to Sunday worship, only to die a few weeks later from pneumonia. We might have an Uncle Pete, whose religious concerns were nil, but whose spiritual values were stirred when the unconditional care given him by his daughter-in-law prepared him for his death by cancer.

Then there is the legendary character, an Aunt Rosie, the happy-go-lucky shopping addict who left her mop and bucket in the middle of the kitchen floor when an invitation to "shop" was offered. With few exceptions, parents hold a very special place among those listed as "family." When challenges hit, they usually meet the demands of change by their long hours of work in fields, factories, offices, hospitals, or wherever. Their trust in God, in themselves, in new approaches to old problems, all form a treasured legacy. Families usually give good example, but sometimes they give less-than-good example. In any case, they probably did their best, and we are left with a valuable relational legacy.

In this twenty-first century, the concept of family has changed. No longer do we define ourselves as a nuclear unit composed of two parents and their children. Blended families, extended families are still families in the relational sense. But the boundaries, roles, responsibilities can have a different meaning, function, and form. History assures us that the definition of the family's organization has always been changing. And it will continue to change. That is the nature of family. Hanging on to "old ways" when new ways work better, is counter-productive. Refusing to define family in relational rather than in biological terms no longer works.

Carlos, the only son of poor immigrant parents, got caught up in an inner-city gang during his freshman year in high school. Although academically talented, he was on his way to failure, and a destructive social network. During this confusing, painful adolescent experience, one of Carlos' teachers noticed his growing belligerent attitude, his drop-out behavior. The quality time and genuine care that Ms. O'Neill invested in Carlos eventually paid off. After serving a jail sentence for a gang-related disturbance, he changed direction, graduated high school, completed graduate level studies, earned his Ph.D. and went on to provide educational and psychological help for "kids at risk." Carlos' life-change was due to what we might call a family affair. Not simply parental support, but in his case, extended, non-biological family support encouraged his about-face change of direction. Family is about life-engendering, relational connections. For many of us, very significant life changes become possible when we can feel the support, caring, and solidarity of family affirmation.

When youth meets the challenges of change, hope in humanity feels renewed. What are the hopes we have for later-life changes? At age eighty-one, Fanny is far from being a "spring chicken." When circumstances mandated her move to a retirement community, she was not a happy camper. After all the fuss and fury of her stubborn refusal to give up home, lifestyle, and familiar surroundings, Fanny finally found herself in a new place, with new routines, new neighbors, new everything. These major changes shook the foundations of her once complacent soul.

"You can't teach an old dog, new tricks." This common wisdom may hold true for canines, but senior living does not cater to "old dogs." At the invitation of her new friends, with the support of staff and residents, Fanny came around to accepting—and enjoying—her unwanted life change. After almost two years, she often remarks that her new home "feels like the gateway to heaven." Accepting and enjoying change does not just happen. Supportive relationships, caring "family" are always somehow involved. At every major turning point in our lives, we can probably find treasured remembrances of those who came into our lives and "familied" us toward our productive decisions of change and renewal.

Solidarity is a holistic experience of communal connection. It affirms our personal value, assuring us of a healthful togetherness, and challenges our growth potential. As a human concept it is comforting and empowering. But solidarity has another dimension, another part of it that keeps solidarity from becoming mindless, soulless, and purposeless. What keeps solidarity in balance? Solitude! Given the fear or discomfort generated by the very thought of solitude, it would be easy to conclude that extroverts reign supreme. Our disregard, our lack of appreciation for solitude's value—even its necessity—owes much to Western cultural conditioning.

Solitude shares equal value with solidarity. Both are gifts that deserve respectful incorporation into our daily routine. Before he began his ministry, Jesus spent many days in solitude. In Mark 1: 35, we find that "In the morning, while it was still very dark, he got up and went out to a deserted place, and there he prayed." A spiritually sensitive way of life does not take away our need of solitude. Nor does it promise to keep us immune from feelings of loneliness—that loneliness that can remind us of Life beyond life. During his last week, the days we call "holy," Jesus experienced the depths of loneliness. In our own experiences of loneliness, we too must follow our Model, and trust beyond "reason's logic." Prayerfully, intuitively we come to know that only God can satisfy our inmost yearnings for completion. No family, no friend, no community, no work, no "thing" can keep us from bouts of loneliness. This loneliness, this poverty of spirit, allows God to fill up our emptiness.

During my tenure as a marriage and family therapist, I found that too many marriage problems were sourced in the false premise that a partner could prevent feelings of loneliness. The stress fueled by this misconception has caused unnecessary pain and ruin to relationships and families beyond count. In solitude, loneliness gets identified for what it is: an opportunity to change, to open our minds and hearts to God's unconditional love.

Communal Belonging

Without the life-giving empowerment of solitude, solidarity dies. Without the wise insights birthed in the pregnant quiet of aloneness, communal living cannot flourish. When she relocated because of her new job opportunity, Dori brought her can-do approach to life with her. As a forty-five year old single Mom, with professional competence, a generous heart, and a desire for meaningful social relationships, she wholeheartedly gave herself to family, work, and church. Shortly after getting settled, she got word of her mother's sudden death. This marked the onset of Dori's severely increased back pain. Soon, the medical decision was made that she would have surgery on her back, and this would be followed by two weeks of complete rest. Immediately, church members rallied to her support. They offered all kinds of help: meals, errands, friendly visits, and so on. Although grateful for their many kindnesses, Dori was surprised that her friends' help felt rather intrusive, less than comforting. At first she could not get a clear read on her preference for alone time, on her dread of even one more visitor. Then during her early morning moments for prayerful reading, she came across a thought by Henri Nouwen. According to him, solitude and community stand together.

To build a viable supportive community, we must allow freedom and space among people, so that we do not cling together, so that we do not fear loneliness. In solitude we open ourselves "to the liberating voice of God." Nouwen's vision of Christian community makes time and space for us to be silent together. This is "a silence in which together we pay attention to the Lord who calls us together. In this way we come to know each other, not as people who cling anxiously to our self-constructed identity, but as people who are loved by the same God in a very intimate and unique way." This is real communal solidarity, a togetherness within which we discover our inwardness, our solitude that is not empty, but is filled with God's fullness.

As we have seen, a healthful productive lifestyle involves change of every kind: personal, spiritual, communal, relational. For a good example of how this life dynamic meets reality, the gospels point out how shared communal meals were a most distinctive part of Jesus' ministry. His inclusive approach to community won him great criticism from Scribes and Pharisees. "Why does he eat with tax collectors and sinners?" (Mark 2:16) Given the strict religious code of his day which excluded the "undesirables," the marginalized outcasts of society, Jesus' meal practice was inclusive, and a big change from the usual protocol. As Borg and Crossan remind us in *The Last Week*, Jesus' dining habits were not meant to be simply symbolic of solidarity, or community. They were real inclusive meals!

Anyone familiar with the Mediterranean cultures can tell you how important food is for connection and well-being. Visiting my Italian relatives was always a time of togetherness, and of "mange!" My Italian grandmother's most familiar saying was "mange!" It was easy to make her smile: just "mange." And this food sharing, this eating together helped to solidify family, friends, neighbors, visitors. All were accepted at our table. This was a taken-for-granted habit.

Jesus' final meal on Thursday of Holy Week was not simply a symbolic gesture. It was about "participation in Christ," about sharing earth's gifts in justice, peace, and caring community. Jesus calls us to a fundamental change, "from bondage to liberation, and participation in the path that leads through death to new life." This communal meal nourishes body, mind, and spirit. This way of sharing changes, heals, and empowers all participants to go and tell others, "what the Lord had done for you, and how kind he has been to you." (Mark 5:19)

In the "narcissistic" days of my youth, I never had the least concern about who would get, cook, and serve the great meals of our family get-togethers. It was always delicious, always plentiful, and always taken-for-granted. Because of their tender years, children are easily forgiven their egocentric ways. However, they are often intuitively wise. They know without any coaching that each person contributes something to the family celebration by his or her own unique presence. Community is more than the sum of its individual members. But that something more depends on the quality, the authenticity, the peace that each individual radiates. Have you ever been in a group, or committee in which one person exhibits a negative, argumentative presence? Unfortunately, it takes only one person sorely lacking in people skills to dampen group enthusiasm, to disrupt communal sharing. It is one thing to understand cognitively that "he has an attitude." It is something else to feel the discomforting presence of that person's negative, disruptive presence.

This issue of individual presence and communal belonging is no easily dismissed concern. As adult persons, we owe our families of origin, our extended "families," and our other nurturing communities, the "love, justice, and power" that marks us as growing, thriving persons. Without individual commitment to holistic development, without the fullness of our authentic personal and spiritual presence, our sharing with others remains lacking in power to comfort and heal.

Healing Moments

1. Take a few minutes to sit quietly, and to breathe deeply.
2. Identify those special persons in your biological or extended family who have shown you significant love, understanding, and support.
3. In gratitude, embrace them spiritually and tell them how important they have been, and continue to be in your life.
4. Open yourself to God's love which you were able to feel through their agency.
5. Stay with this comforting love as you continue to breathe deeply and slowly.
6. Place yourself, body-mind-spirit, in the presence of God whose unconditional love is always with you. Resolve to be more mindful of the Divine Presence.

Getting Stuck in Family Roles

Whether we realize it or not, the customs and culture of family life are not easily changed—or even challenged. Long standing influences leave indelible imprints in the cognitive tissue of the human brain. Both conscious and unconscious learning leaves encoded mandates that are not easily erased. To help us get beyond the constricting "should" and "ought," and beyond other useless "musts," a little honest reflection on family rules and roles can help clear the way for productive change.

First, rules are necessary for good order and group comfort. This holds true for any kind of family structure, for large institutions, for religious groups, for every kind of human togetherness. But, when rules are too vague, or inconsistent, then disruptive confusion can result. On the other hand, when rules describing ways for relational interactions become lost in prescriptive absolutes, then productive change is a long way off.

Second, informed conscience, along with determined effort are required for the continuing developmental changes that are our natural birthright. When any segment within the various kinds of family systems finds the need for change, significant challenges are close at hand. In the more dysfunctional systems, needs for even modest change are met with increased rigidity, with more stubborn determination to maintain "the rules"—even if they are no longer relevant. When this "stuckness" happens between the individual who sees the need for change, and the family that opts for no-change, this resulting conflict can become brutal—even deadly. In his history of *The Reformation*, Diarmaid MacCulloch gives us his scholarly research on the wars and suffering in the Middle Ages. During these terrible times, institutional "families" fought to the death (literally) against change.

In today's postmodern age, do we seem to be any more civilized? Some would say, "No!" We still have not given sufficient evidence that we understand and accept our need for inward growth and development, for an ability to meet the challenges of change whether they come to our "families" or ourselves.

Returning again to Jesus, our Model, when he admonished his listeners to go beyond the righteousness of the Scribes and Pharisees, he was not trashing these learned and observant Jews. John Meier, in his Volume II of *The Marginal Jew*, reminds us that in general the Pharisees were a somewhat sophisticated urban movement which demanded of its members a certain level of scholarly learning and discipline of life. Usually a Pharisee had enough leisure and financial security to engage in "regular study and punctilious practice of the law." They were rule-keepers with very definite ideas and practices relating to purity, divorce, tithing, and other Jewish observations. Jesus had his own different perspective, one that took him beyond the Law. He saw a need for change, for new and sometimes disturbing rules about accepted observances. Jesus was not afraid of a spiritual growth change. Nor must we be!

Among my many learning moments is the realization that our understanding of human good is limited rather than absolute, and consequently, it obliges us to consistently correct our limited perspective. In other words, be prepared to meet the many changes that life demands. On the issue of changing the accepted ideas about discipleship, Elizabeth Schussler Fiorenza began one of her theological presentations by relating her personal encounter with patriarchy. After Fiorenza completed her Master of Divinity degree, she was assured that if the Vatican II Council approved their decision, she would be recommended for ordination. However, she did not feel called to pastoral work as such, but rather to a teaching leadership position as bishop. She was immediately told, "That will never happen!" Why? "Because then we (men) would depend on you, and owe obedience to you." Here we find no willingness within the Church leadership to get beyond the rule, or to see more deeply into its purpose as Jesus did. Church leadership showed no willingness to appropriately adapt to the necessity of change.

Beyond family or organizational rules and expectations, the demands of a well-lived life call us to engage fully, to invest wisely in who we are becoming. This may at times mean that we meet the status quo with our honest, insightful, observations and questions. Refusing to challenge rigid, harmful rules and established protocol is not an option. God's legacy of love, and God's intention for human wholeness is rooted in creative change.

As a concerned Christian, I must insist on a change in many Church policies, especially in those rules that keep women and men subservient and "battered." Jesus was clearly for any change that might improve our lives, bring us peace of mind and heart, and deepen our connection with God. In our postmodern global village, family takes on a more diversified, extended meaning.

Occupational hazards come in all kinds of forms and circumstances. Getting stuck in our various personal and professional roles is an example of a very stressful predicament. Jon Kabot-Zinn points out that any roles, whether they be from work, group, professional, social, or other sources, all limit us when we have little or no understanding of the damage they can do. His research confirms the fact that "Role stress is a side effect of our ingrained habits of doing when the domain of being gets lost. It can be a major obstacle to our continued psychological growth and the source of much frustration and suffering." Many of our social and professional roles carry implied expectations about what it means to be a good parent, friend, educator, business person, physician, nurse, priest or minister, and so forth. Perhaps unwittingly, or perhaps willingly, we allow an aura of exaggerated importance, authority, or power to be attached to roles. For example, a physician's white coat, or a military uniform can carry more significance than is warranted. We do ourselves a great disservice when we let unconscious expectations dictate the way we express or value ourselves.

The practice of mindfulness can help us to get beyond the damaging effects of role stress. The tyranny of many experiences of stress too often comes from our unawareness, distractions, or misperceptions. An effective antidote for taking the "steam" out of role stress involves the practice of mindfulness, that same kind of alertness that Jesus calls us to practice. If we can bring our keen awareness to examine experiences of role stress, then we are more likely to accomplish our roles without getting stuck in them, without getting caught in the narcissistic net of self-importance, of egocentric authoritarianism.

From a holistic perspective, any stressful circumstance can be influenced by our own perspectives, by our own ability to go with the flow of change. Having a negative mindset exacerbates the stressful experience, makes a "mountain out of a mole hill," and interferes with productive resolution. But this does not need to be the case. Instead of experiencing the downside of automatic role stress, we can turn the obstacles encountered into opportunities for personal and spiritual growth.

After enduring many years of relational stress, Jim and Marcia sought relief from their conflicted marriage. In spite of having a successful business career behind him, neither Jim nor Marcia looked forward to retirement. Caught in his work role, and being heavily analytic in his perceptions, Jim helped to polarize his relationship with Marcia whose career as a nurse locked her into synthesizing perspectives. Psychotherapy helped them see how they were causing their own relational stress. To help them get beyond their discomfort, they agreed to: a) commit to the practice of mindfulness; b) make their under-functioning brain hemisphere more operative. A few weeks later, they returned for their scheduled therapy session. Jim was elated: Marcia was taking a philosophy course at the local university. And Jim? When asked what he was doing to improve his synthesizing skills, Jim's facial expression said, "Why would anyone need to expand right-brain skills?"

Jim's polarizing effect on his marriage involved both his work role attachment, and his over-functioning left-brain analytic skills. On the other hand, Marcia's attachment to her nurturing role had her wanting in left-brain thinking. The postmodern cultural preference for left-brain analysis over right-brain synthesis, distorts the needed balance of full personal involvement in relational dialogue and bonding. Change saved their relationship!

Healing Moments

1. Gift yourself with several quiet moments. Relax. Breathe deeply.
2. Mentally review your designated role in your biological family, church community, and extended social groups.
3. Ask yourself if this role encourages you to grow personally and spiritually.
4. If you are uncomfortable about any relational role, turn inward to your spiritual center.
5. Recall the example of your spiritual Model, and how he lived and grew beyond the accepted roles of his cultural environment.
6. In loving trust, place yourself in the creative embrace of the Ultimate Reality that can empower you to grow beyond any role constraints.
7. Commit yourself to personal and spiritual renewal.

Spirituality and the Elephant Tracks

"Don't follow the elephant tracks." I first heard this expression in Father Burns' college religion class. Being a naïve freshman coed, I waited expectantly to hear what he meant. Father Burns was a famous campus faculty character, known as an excellent teacher who had an unconventional approach to education. His main objective was to "get the wheels turning." This he did as only he could, with good humor, dramatic tales, and always probing questions. He did not want us to mimic the lemmings, those little grey furry mouse-like creatures that mindlessly ran with the crowd, and eventually plunged headlong over a precipice to their death. Father Burns believed in rules; he believed even more in creative change.

When the history of his Main Line University boasted of all male students, he did not see that as good enough reason to prohibit an open-door policy for full-time women students. Fast-forward from the 1950's to now when his campus has blossomed into a first-rate seat of co-educational learning. He lived his own commitment to change, and tried to prepare his students for the challenge by getting their "wheels turning." For him the good life meant growth; growth meant change; change meant getting our mind in gear before we moved in any direction. Change involved every part of who we are. Factual data about "out there" keeps us well informed. However, if we are to make our own path through life, if we are to avoid following the Elephant Tracks of mindless journeying, then we must look "inward."

Spirituality has sometimes been labeled, "soft pathology." This is an unfair, but understandable criticism. If the introspection of spirituality is used as an escape route from reality, neurosis or worse makes itself known. When a well-meaning aspirant to seminary was referred to me for counseling, problems of self-identity surfaced almost immediately. Although in her mid-fifties, this woman was still functioning at an adolescent's developmental level. She was not yet able to be comfortable with paradox, compromise, or change.

Seeds of growth, sown in formative years need time to take root, to emerge in the mature years. If platitudes, ideology, and absolutes reign supreme, then the possibility of gaining insights and courage remains dormant. One of the joys of the ageing process (and humanly speaking there aren't many) is the inner wisdom that sees "success" as the pretentious promise it is, that values truth and compassion far beyond clever accomplishments.

In *Wisdom: From Philosophy to Neuroscience*, Stephen Hall writes: "One of the hallmarks of wisdom, what distinguishes it so sharply from 'mere' intelligence, is the ability to exercise good judgment in the face of imperfect knowledge." Many retirees support the evidence for this view of wisdom, while at the same time they acknowledge another distinguishing characteristic: wisdom's spiritual dimension. And if there is a truism that crosses all cultures "from Confucianism to the loving kindness of Jesus, it is that wisdom does not come easily." The personal, spiritual wisdom that comes with years of life experience does not simply fall upon us like the gentle rain. It requires the discipline of mindfulness in the present moment, openness to the challenge of change, and courage to trust the Spirit deep within us.

What practical advantage do ageing adults enjoy because of their wisdom, gleaned through the years? Again, referring to Hill's study, "Adults between the ages of sixty and eighty think more strategically (and successfully) to solve problems, both impersonal intellectual problems, and interpersonal social problems." This, as we know, is hardly news. Many centuries ago Cicero reminded us that qualities of thought, character, and judgment actually increase with age. In some ways wisdom favors older adults, many of whom have developed a feel for solutions to a problem. They know from experience the value of tapping into emotional, holistic intuition, and their right-brain capabilities. According to Hill's sources, being wise suggests not only an honest gleaning of knowledge, but also the spiritual gift of discernment. These essential qualities help to make us wise. They are repeatedly mentioned in the Old Testament as being "divine in origin but rooted in an understanding of human nature."

Scripture tells us that wisdom comes with old age. We have the Biblical examples of Abraham, Job, Salomon, and others. In Hebrew, the word for wisdom includes the fact of a mind-body connection. From both a spiritual and a psychological perspective, there are sufficient empirical studies to strongly suggest three general areas of concern to the study of wisdom: cognitive, affective, and intuitive. The more holistically human experiences we have, the greater our chances for becoming wise. The ageing process does not have much to recommend it, according to popular opinion, but certainly, having an inside line to wisdom is a most valuable opportunity for on-going growth and well-being, no matter one's age.

When death marked the end of over fifty years of marriage, Mona mourned her great loss, accepted the transitional discomforts, healed her inner wounds of change, and offered her friendly support to those struggling with similar challenges. Why, at her advanced age, was she able to meet so effectively those life changes that test our wisdom and courage? Evidently, she was not an Elephant Tracks traveler. Her inner spiritual identity did not depend on human limitations. She knew and accepted herself as being "in process" of growth. And she believed in her value as a person, irrespective of any family, organizational connections. Since the spiritual dimension of her life was foundational to her sense of identity, she was not unduly limited by others' expectations. Through expanded consciousness and compassionate sensitivity, Mona's senior years proved to be a gift of time. While the yearnings and strivings of early adulthood often keep us trudging along the Elephant Tracks, Mona traveled her own happy path of wisdom and peace. Through her good humor and friendly manner she followed Jesus' mandate to share with others the joy and wisdom of God's way.

Before taking a closer look at additional ways of avoiding the Elephant Tracks trap, and of developing our personal and spiritual capabilities for renewal, a helpful clarification is in order: Meeting the challenges of change, healing the wounds we sustain, living productively even into advanced years, is a do-it-yourself job. As already suggested, it is up to us to become aware, stay alert, develop skills, and accept support. Sometimes (perhaps more often than not) our "becoming" has the comfort index of a net-less, high wire tight rope walk. However, in this case God's goodness—or if you prefer, the wisdom of the Universe—enfolds and sustains our every effort.

Everything is Grace

How we choose to maintain our honest introspection and faithful practice depends on our level of consciousness, honesty, and sensitivity. Looking back on my own efforts of self-understanding and meaningful meditation, I am reminded of the many mentors who generously shared their life-learned wisdom. My own decades of asking, searching, and knocking have convinced me that "everything is grace."

Years ago I came across a little paperback book by Joe Hyams. I asked myself, "Why in the world would I want to read a book about *Zen in the Martial Arts?*" It did not take me long to appreciate the wisdom behind its directives for thoughtful discipline, and for ways of being spiritually awake. In his section on going with the flow of life, Hyams quotes Lao Tzu: "Softness triumphs over hardness, feebleness over strength. What is more malleable is always superior over that which is immoveable." In different words, in a different context, Jesus said much the same thing when he spoke of the meek inheriting the earth.

And again, in order to gain honest introspection and faithful practice, we are called to appropriate discipline, without which there is no peace. From the Bhagavad Gita, Hyams quotes, "For the uncontrolled there is no wisdom, nor for the uncontrolled is there the power of concentration; and without concentration there is no peace. And for the unpeaceful, how can there be happiness?" Here too, Jesus admonishes us to be alert, to be wise, and to be peaceful.

In helping to broaden our consciousness, in deepening our sensitivity, the wisdom of the world's great religions can help to increase our love and appreciation of the Christian message. Although the Quaker background of Thomas Merton may have remotely influenced him in his decision to live the contemplative life of a Christian monk, he did not abandon "the world." In fact, he became deeply committed to sharing the Christian message with his brothers and sisters the world over. He was a no-nonsense, cut-to-the-chase writer and teacher. He practiced what he preached. In his meditations on *The Way of Chuang Tzu*, Merton wrote that we ought not to worry about what we should do, and what we should not do in any particular situation. Since there is no fixed absolute answer to the wisest choice of action, our focus needs to be on the spirit-centered life. Then with our awareness of God's presence, right action will make itself known as the circumstances require. Merton reminds us that although Chuang Tzu lacks the profoundly theological mysticism of St. Paul, "this Eastern teaching is not far removed from St. Paul's teaching about faith and grace."

If in the course of our everyday circumstances, we open ourselves to the grace-filled opportunity of the present moment, then there will be no clinging to partial, exclusive opinions. The person who is grounded in grace has become comfortably familiar with an inner spontaneous obedience to the Holy Spirit. Compassion, devoted love, and sincerity, along with other teachings of Jesus like simplicity, childlikeness, and humility are all marks of wisely lived commitments. In his brief introduction to *The Way of Chuang Tzu*, Merton reminds us that a core message of the gospel is complemented by Chuang Tzu: To lose one's life is to save it, and to seek to save it for one's own sake is to lose it. The truly wise person would agree with St. John of the Cross that when we enter into Jesus's way, we do well to leave the Elephant Tracks, and to trust in the Spirit's guidance. We can open ourselves to the unfamiliar because everything is grace.

Reflective Moments

1. How have your family connections helped or hindered your efforts to grow (change) as a developing person? What kinds of support did they give you when you needed encouragement? Why are separations so necessary, yet so painful?
2. In Mark 1:35 we are told that in the morning while it was still very dark, Jesus got up and went to a deserted place, and there he prayed. How does your way of living a meaningful, spiritual life allow for necessary and prayerful solitude?
3. Jesus had perspectives about meaningful growth and creative change that took him beyond the Law. How do you accept the need for change of rules, or of accepted protocol?
4. Since meeting the many challenges of change that come your way requires awareness, skills, and support, how much energy, thought, and prayer do you put into your personal and spiritual growth process?
5. Throughout his life, Jesus showed by his example that flexibility was more desirable than rigidity, and that compassion was better than insensitivity. How have you attempted to avoid the Elephant Tracks, and to accept your own creative challenges?
6. Refusing to accept change keeps us victims of our immature habits. In what specific ways do you open yourself to the challenge of change, and to your own need for continual growth and development?

5.

MOVE BEYOND THE FEARS AND ANXIETIES OF CHANGE

"The Spirit of Truth will guide you into everything that is true."
(John 16:13)

Developmental Challenges of Change

Developing into a fully functioning personality does not just happen. In a very real sense "we grow ourselves." We do this in our post-adolescent deliberations by knowing and accepting who we are, by choosing to interact productively in all our relationships with self, others, environment, and Reality. We become who we are through these dynamic relationships, these experiences of both stability and change. But it is not our experiences alone that help to form us. It is what we do with these challenges of sameness and newness.

Even for those considered "privileged," individual initiative is still required for healthful development. As a complacent freshman in a private convent high school for girls, I gave into the temptation to sneak a look at my private (for Sister's eyes only) student file. But curiosity was not satisfied. What did it mean: "She is not using all her talents and abilities." Confusion filled my brain. What was expected of me? What more could I do? Environmentally, I was in a good place. But what was I going to do with these formative experiences? This was, and remained the big question.

A nurturing environment is an essential ingredient for personal and spiritual development. But that does not mean comfort zones are an absolute. In fact, they can be negative forces if they interfere with a person's differentiation, autonomy, and full development. Feeling always comforted might result in fusion with the nurturing "family." A dangerous connection for both the person and the group! Getting beyond this temptation to "dig in," and to stay within the comfort zone, calls for change. Change in perspectives, in decisiveness, in direction!

However, simplistic approaches to personal and spiritual development are anathema. In *The Evolving Self*, Robert Kegan cautions that development is not just about actualization, individuation. It is about the integration of the individual and the group, a kind of "marriage" in which independence and interdependence form a smoothly functioning relationship.

Once again, family as a paradigm for change gives us a close-up picture of how perniciously static mind-sets can prevent healthful personal and spiritual growth. In psychotherapeutic parlance, a person's enmeshment in family organization blurs legitimate, appropriate boundaries between and among the individual members. This results in over-involvement, in their "breathing out of each other's lungs." Even with little imagination, the claustrophobic atmosphere can easily be identified as damaging—even lethal. If not thwarted, the natural impulse to break away, to walk one's own path, sets in motion the healthful inclination to respond to life's new complexities in one's own distinctive way, to welcome qualitative change, and to relate more effectively to self, others, and to Ultimate Reality.

The balance between differentiation and integration, between autonomy and inclusion, between solitude and solidarity is probably one of the most significant change-challenges we will ever face. It is so basic that it is usually missed, or misunderstood.

Human perfection does not exist. But with "good enough" growth opportunities, personal and spiritual development can move forward, and individuals can live "good lives." When fear and anxiety intrude on our relational experiences, these unwelcome feelings could be a wake-up call, a warning indicator. Change, transition, and loss test our mettle, let us know about developmental lags, or weak spots along our growth line. Any trip-up in our multi-dimensional make-up, any blockage in our cognitive, emotive, intuitive system will have negative repercussions in our everyday experiences.

Steve, an in-charge guy, an on-top-of-things leader fell into a black hole of confusion, fear, and anxiety when his accounting business went belly-up. As a skilled numbers-man, his abilities ranked second to none. But not-so his people skills! For him, understanding how a trusted employee could embezzle funds from the business, or could betray Steve's trust was off the charts, beyond his comprehension. At the insistence of family, Steve invested in several months of psychotherapy. There he took a "family journey" into his developmental years, and there he clarified his unconscious refusal to admit an unrealistic idealism that kept him from seeing the truth.

Steve's formative years were filled with the pain of significant relational anxieties, especially with his father's abusive alcoholic behavior, and his mother's neurotic co-dependent refusal to admit their family was not perfect. Re-investing in himself, in his value as an autonomous person took time and effort. Eventually he "thanked" his loss, his fear and anxiety for forcing him to seek professional help. He was then able to see the value and advantage for his personal change.

As a gift of Nature, fear keeps children afraid of the dark, of snakes, of spiders and other dangers. Moving into adolescence, we find different but still significant objects or situations to protectively discomfort us. If our growth trajectory goes well, by adulthood life's fears and anxieties stimulate but no longer overwhelm us. Instead, in the best circumstances, they push us forward toward change and resolution. But circumstances are not always the best. A well-researched statistic suggests very sobering data: In the USA over 60% of adults have an emotional maturity level of a 16 year old adolescent.

Culture has a lot to answer for! But so do adults who refuse to acknowledge and accept the challenges of change, who fear the natural ageing process, who live with unexamined psychological and spiritual discomforts or anxieties. Enhanced living at every age, under any circumstances, demands a courageous openness to the challenges of change.

The human developmental process is not without its painful demands. Growth is hardly ever easy. Why? It demands that we leave behind us old familiar ways of thinking and acting. Living with our own specific limitations, recognizing the finitude of our existence can in itself open us to fears and anxieties. But we do real damage to ourselves when we defend against openness, change, and renewal. Any determination we make against the natural flow of life will cause us pain. When we defend ourselves against the changes that loss brings, when we try to by-pass our feelings of grief or our need to mourn, then we are "self-abusive." We are allowing the more painful experience of unexamined anxiety to out-do the normal discomfort of change itself.

How do we know that our developmental change, or our dealing with the losses involved in the growth process, will be worth the struggle? Jesus reminds us that the fruits of our efforts will answer that question. In other words, if we are more comfortable with ourselves and others, if we are more natural and spontaneous in our behavior, if we can laugh at our own foibles and are more patient with human limitations, and if we are more creatively open to life's spiritual dimension, then we have a least the beginning of an answer to our question. These are comforting thoughts. However, they do not satisfy our need to know how we might avoid or mitigate the pot-holes of fear and anxiety that we face along the developmental path.

In our most challenging circumstances, self-understanding is always helpful. Our unique genetic predispositions usually offer opportunities for insight. For example, a natural predisposition toward certain personal characteristics might be considered an asset or a liability depending on one's life-stage, and the immediate circumstances. Should "stubbornness" be viewed as an ornery, or a strong-minded characteristic?

I vividly recall my life as a seven year old, in suburban Bucks County. We little folks found easy delight on a lazy summer afternoon, playing a relaxed game of wire-ball. Dave, a new kid to our neighborhood appeared on the scene flaunting his brand new two-wheeler bike, with its bell, fancy gadgets, and more. At nine years of age, he was already feeling a bit macho in the company of my seven (girl) years. Brief conversation between us led to a bet. "I can ride my bike full speed from the top of the hill, straight at you, and make you get out of my way." "Bet you can't make me move!" "Yes I can!" "No you can't!" "Bet you a dime I can!" "It's a bet that you can't!" Within minutes, he came barreling down the hill straight at me while furiously ringing his new bell. I stubbornly stood my ground! Unable to stop, he biked directly into me, knocked me down, and then fell spread-eagle in one direction while his new bike scraped its way across the loose street cinders, in the opposite direction. My knees were a bloody mess. Dave, shocked at my refusal to move, kept repeating, "But I told you to move!" I doubt that he ever heard my clear response: "And I told you I would not move!" I can't remember whether he ever gave me the dime I won.

I look back from my present day vantage point, and smile indulgently at my stubborn immaturity. At that point in my life, I had not yet learned the wisdom of compromise, or flexibility. Nor could I then appreciate the pre-puberty need for strutting—either Dave's or my own. And yet with proper guidance, the determination to stand one's ground would eventually lead to developmental maturity.

Self-Love Without Apology

In our honest efforts to get beyond the challenging fears and anxieties that block our path to personal and spiritual peace, we can always be encouraged by Jesus' assurance that "The Spirit of truth will guide you into everything that is true." (John 16:13) Yet, why do we turn away so often from a fundamental truth concerning ourselves? We speak and write eloquently about compassion, about the need to care deeply for all others within our human community. Yet we seem to feel uncomfortable with the need to care deeply and truly for ourselves. In *Twelve Steps to a Compassionate Life*, Karen Armstrong tells the story of a Jewish rabbi who stressed the love-commandment: "Love your neighbor as yourself." (Leviticus 19:18) As a young boy growing up amidst the fears and anxieties rampant in anti-Semitic Nazi Germany, Albert would deliberately lay awake at night listing his good qualities. He refused to believe he was the terrible, worthless person the Nazis said he was. He believed he had talents and spiritual gifts of heart and mind, which he enumerated to himself one-by-one. Albert survived the Nazi camps, and lived to help and counsel many who faced their own life's anxieties and fears. However, he was convinced that his compassionate support of others would not be possible unless he had learned to love himself.

The Golden Rule, by any definition, requires self-knowledge, and self-acceptance. This involves our honesty about both our weaknesses and our strengths. Neither our positive qualities, nor our negative ones can in any way diminish our value as persons who carry within us the Spirit of Life. This is the Source of our dignity which no one can take from us.

So why do we minimize our true worth by engaging in neurotic tendencies that diminish our self-appreciation. Why can we not reflect seriously on Jesus' assurance that the kingdom of God is within us? Yes, we are valued persons in spite of our misdeeds, or negative behaviors. True, we must accept responsibility for our actions even when they originate in the primitive, reflex reactions of the "reptilian brain" where automatic fears, and anxieties under-mind the truth of our God-given value.

But these negative experiences cannot lessen our true identity as members of God's human family. Certain kinds of challenges can scare the bejeebees out of us, and can leave us feeling like spineless cowards. What do we do then? We show great compassion toward our selves! We might even follow Albert's example and remind ourselves that our faults cannot take away or diminish our human dignity. When I find myself caught in the trap of mental or physical limitations, I find it helpful to remember that I did not ask for my cognitive, and bodily "liabilities." My challenge involves understanding and accepting who I am; it involves knowing that my feelings of fear and anxiety are part of the human condition. An attitude of true compassion toward ourselves, and a trust in Life's unfathomable ways can help us to become liberated from our inner wounds, and to more fully accept who we are.

We know that love has healing power. So, in very practical terms, what does our self-loving, self-healing process involve? Hope is essential! Without the hope that there is more to life than meets the eye, without trust in life's spiritual dimension, self-appreciation can hardly get off the ground. But self-esteem, as a personal, spiritual quality needs nurturing. Like Albert, we too must find ways to foster a deep respect and appreciation for we are. This calls for both an informed conscience, and an emotional acceptance of who we are. It calls for fewer negative feelings about our self, and a closer relationship with God. Supportive friends, and loving family can all help to advance our healing work, our efforts toward full-scale, compassionate living.

In learning to love ourselves properly, and without apology, we are brought back again to a consideration of what it means to have compassion for our self. Partly because of our post-modern obsession with achievement, most of us have difficulty accepting our shortcomings and under-achievements. Cover-ups for personal "failures" can take the form of several common self-hate maneuvers: addictions to food, drugs, work, sex, exercise, stuff, and more. At his center for stress reduction, Jon Kabot-Zinn never tires of reminding the participants that they are not their pain; their true personal value cannot be measured by feelings of fear and anxiety. God does not make junk. Our personal value remains beyond dispute.

Yes, positive attitudes have much to recommend them. But life has its seasons. Holy Scripture reminds us of times to be joyful, of times to be sorrowful. Mourning our losses is a natural part of the human condition. Our grieving rituals help heal our loss wounds. During this challenging process, we gain insight, humility, courage, and empowerment to love ourselves. With the same sense of compassionate caring that we give to ourselves, we can then give to others.

Healing Moments

1. Sit quietly for several moments. Relax. Breathe deeply.
2. Call to mind times of fear, anxiety, or general discomfort from your past.
3. Admit your discomfort without condemning yourself in any way, for anything.
4. Allow yourself to fully accept those unwelcome, painful experiences.
5. Fully accept your feelings, whatever they may be. They are a valuable part of you.
6. Compassionately embrace all of yourself, and thank God for the gift of you.

Seeing the Wisdom of Our Discontents

Our birth was the first of many change experiences waiting to challenge and discomfort us. From the no-stress, warm environment of mother's womb, we were forcibly ejected into the noisy, rough world of people. The birthing process is a normal mammalian rite of passage, an often taken-for-granted gift of Nature. But only human beings can boast of a consciousness that supports awareness of meaning, purpose—and yes, wise discontents.

Ted and Alice were first-time parents trying to support themselves during the dreary years of the Great Depression. No government aid or support programs relieved empty stomachs or survival worries. They had their extended family, but like countless others, Ted and Alice had legitimate, serious discontents. These experiences were light-years away from a human life, lived in the worry-free, effort-free, stress-free world of mother's womb. Post-natal reality with its never-ending pinches and pokes, gives us every reason to complain, to defend against discomforting intrusions.

But contrary to any "negative press" our discontents have an up-side, a tendency toward beneficence. Discontents do us good when they shake and shatter the complacency of automatic acceptance, of our status quo absolutes. Pages of history hold highly valued stories of heroic individuals who met their discontents head-on, leaving a legacy of wisdom and empowerment. Benedict founded Western Monasticism; Montaigne gave us the literary essay; Siddhartha gave us Buddhism, and most significantly, Jesus gave us a "good news" relationship with God.

Taking a close-up look at our discontents brings together challenge and reward. A little digging into legitimate dissatisfactions uncovers a few possible causes: habits of stale conformity, fear of being different, adherence to useless platitudes, refusal to think inclusively, lack of self-appreciation. Sleuthing around for sound understanding disallows our moaning, groaning excuses. No room here for shame or blame in any direction. There is only room for the clear realization that the way to contentment is "not in the stars," but within our own mind and heart. The wisdom and resolution of our discontents are to be found within ourselves.

In my wild adolescent imagination, especially in times of "misery," I dreamily wondered if Jesus ever entertained any discontents. Did he prefer the more inclusive atmosphere of the coastal cities like Sephorus, where he worked his carpentry jobs? Did the exclusive attitudes and customs of his village life generate respectful discontents, eventually guiding him to his baptism by John the Baptizer? Maybe yes; maybe no! But the fact remains: Our legitimate needs to get beyond constricting relationships, beyond unexamined ideology, call us to acknowledge and understand the genesis of our discontents.

As already mentioned, in Mark's gospel we read about the young man who approached Jesus. Was he too contented with his easy life? In any case he walked away sad, not about to face any inward discontents. On the other hand there was the courageous woman whose discontents led her to Jesus, and to healing. There were many others too, including Bartimaeus whose discontents had him calling out to Jesus, and refusing to be hushed by the crowd. He too found healing for his discontents.

The reasonable constraints of public policy, of religious mandates, of cultural customs, and of family traditions help to protect the early formative stages of human development. But not unlike the baby chick, a breaking-out time comes. Boundaries that once protected us are no longer beneficial. In fact, they have become constructively harmful. Psychological and spiritual "hatching" is an essential need for healthful human development. And it often gets a jump-start by our disturbing discontents.

In connecting the dots between discomforting experiences and their catalytic effects, developmental theorists clarify what we already know. Nature's important work is often advanced by our human discontents. Here again, we are reminded of Kohlberg's moral developmental stages, and Fowler's faith development research.

An awakening of our consciousness changes a "fantasy" world into a real world where self-awareness can develop. In pre-puberty years, we give up literal interpretations of cherished narratives. But the gain of a slowly maturing trust in our own experiences does not come without some real discomforts. In adolescence, an emerging identity allows for a sometimes confusing mix of discomforting change with soothing stability. As maturity evolves human consciousness "hatches." Tensions between individual and communal demands do not evaporate or fade away. Instead they find outlet in valuable myths, and in useful symbols. These constructive myths and symbols, direct our energies toward human liberation.

Unfortunately, this is not the end of a happy story. Too many adult narratives tell about a stubborn preference for unexamined ideology, for excessive and unwarranted confidence in authoritarian determinations. As long as one plus one makes two, "the unexamined life" will be visited by physical, mental, and spiritual discontents that wait to be acknowledged and resolved.

Finding the wisdom in our discontents, helps to uncover and resolve our deep inner needs. And we all have our physical and metaphysical needs. Those who have no needs, no discontents are not among the living. Here is a sobering thought: While dead persons are all equally dead, living persons are not necessarily all equally alive. To be fully alive, deep reflection must be given to our need for change, for attending to those wise discontents. Our needs are by definition worthy concerns that deserve our keen and respectful attention.

Refusal to make use of introspective disciplines like meditation, or personal narrative review, does not win a place on the Smart People list. The examined life may be well worth living, but it does not come with a lifetime warranty against the challenges of change. Within the Christian spiritual tradition, John of the Cross reminds us that when we feel touched by the desire for deeper meaning in our life, discouragement might be nearby.

Continuing to grow psychologically and spiritually increases our sensitivity and sharpens awareness, and shows more clearly the warts and blemishes that we own. Hesitation and refusal to look more closely at the meaning of our discontents, at the necessity of change is understandable. It's just not smart!

For Traci, a single Mom, working full-time, caring for two teen-age daughters, and completing her graduate studies, discontents are high, and reflective moments are few. Reflective moments make sense to her. She requires no convincing about the value—indeed the necessity—of attending to a few significant changes in her life. Dealing with the residual pain of her recent divorce tops her list of challenges. But right now, her morning madness routine does not easily lend itself to introspective moments. Nevertheless, she has transformed her alone time in the shower, into reflective moments that include gratitude for the full flow of clean, warm water, for the sweetly smelling pleasure of her favorite bath gel, for the gift of her body and mind, for the unknown challenges of the coming day, and most especially for each gifted present moment. For Traci, at this stage of her life, five or ten early morning meditative moments in the shower are the best she can do in her efforts to remain in touch with Reality.

Karen's determination to meet the challenges of change is focused more on the ageing process, the attachments and separations that fill her septuagenarian life. Newly retired, bravely dealing with the limitations of rheumatoid arthritis, Karen uses her down-time for meditative reading, for quiet prayer. After a life-time of nurturing others, she is easing into new ways of relating: listening more than telling, allowing "I prefer" instead "I'd be glad to," writing a caring note to a lonely neighbor. Karen admits that not being in charge feels good on some days, bad on others. Change in roles, in perceived identity, though necessary, hardly ever gives a "warm fuzzies" feel. Any change that diminishes our ideal image of our self is worse than threatening—it can feel more like "devastating!"

In later years, change can take on a more unwelcome presence. Bounce-back energy comes slowly, if at all. Putting off, ignoring, or rationalizing the developmental demands of Nature at any point in life, especially in our senior years, can shut down, or seriously inhibit the normal life change process. If we are at least a little honest, our mind-games will not fool us. We are all well-advised not to fool ourselves at any time. Certainly not in the end stages of life!

In-depth psychological studies assure us that any message of legitimate discontent comes to us from the "sacred center" of our being. Its enduring truth tolerates no excuses. The wisdom of our discontents tells us emphatically that meeting the challenge of healthful life changes is not an option. It is a necessity.

Healing Moments

1. Take some time to be quiet. Breathe slowly and deeply.
2. Look inwardly and gently identify a few of your significant discontents.
3. Single out your most challenging discontent, and befriend it. Ask what important message it is trying to tell you.
4. Listen closely to the story that your discontent tells you. Ask it to help you be more accepting of its message. Stay with it for a few friendly moments.
5. Focus on your model (Jesus, Buddha, or your choice) and do not dismiss your discontents. Rather, listen to what they say about the need for change and renewal.
6. Sit peacefully, trustfully with these thoughts while being open to the empowerment of God's, Nature's, and Life's amazing grace.

Legacies of Psychospiritual Change

In *The Way of Transformation*, Karlfried Durckheim encourages us to live our daily lives as a spiritual practice, to expand our human consciousness because in us Divinity becomes conscious of Itself. This is the ultimate, welcome legacy: our dynamic connection with Divinity.

Transformative relationships take us beyond ourselves to incrementally advanced stages of holistic development. As a young five-year-old child, I experienced a startling, powerful, numinous happening that took me to a higher level of consciousness, to a definitive change. In *The Idea of the Holy*, Rudolph Otto says, "Like all other psychical elements, it (the numinous experience) emerges in due course in the developing life of the human mind and spirit, and is thenceforward simply present." And so a deeper consciousness of Reality has stayed with me, growing incrementally as time and circumstances supported my expanding psychospiritual consciousness. This capability for a keen self-awareness, for a more inclusive world view, does not easily happen. It calls for our ability to remain open to any and all transformative changes.

In Robert Coles' book, *The Spirituality of Children*, he shares with his readers the many interviews he had with children who were becoming "God conscious." Pre-puberty children seem less inhibited, more direct in their spiritual narratives. Listening respectfully as Coles did, allows for treasured learning moments no matter the age differential. When Jesus admonished us to take on the ways of childlikeness, he evidently had in mind a child's spontaneous readiness to experience God.

My first wake-up experience of God is as vivid a memory today as it was so many decades ago. It happened in early spring. A carpet of velvety purple violets covered the woodland floor. Held captive by the tiny blossoms, I crawled about, greedily grabbing all the blossoms I could hold. Still on my haunches, and for no particular reason, I turned my head upwards, and squinted at the blinding high noon sun. Blinking, then looking away, I was vividly aware that something powerful, mysterious had happened. What? I didn't have a clue. Speechless, confused, and excited, I ran into the house to tell Mom. But how can "Something happened!" be explained? I groped for words, found none, and gave up trying. All the while baffled by "Something!"

According to Otto, my spiritual consciousness was spontaneously stirred, keenly awakened. To date I am not aware of having been touched in that same enfolding way. Nevertheless, all through these intervening years, that brief, electrifying event still feeds my persistent yearning for transformative encounters with God. Given the where, when, and how of my "awakening," organized religion was hardly, if at all, a causal agent. However, it did play a significant part in my later nurturing requirements of mind and heart.

Our psychological and spiritual growth legacies include, but go far beyond any individual's transformative experience. The values and mores we inherit from our elders and mentors give us virtues to practice, but it is hoped, not idols to worship. All great spiritual, developmental traditions invite us to holistic growth and renewal. In the Christian tradition, Jesus calls us to transformational change through purity of heart and poverty of spirit. Or if you prefer, he calls us to authenticity and responsibility. Healthy individuals are not dualistic; they are holistic. Consequently, all transformational change affects every part of who we are in body, mind, and spirit.

Whether we like it or not, the perennial necessity of change is not going to change! But revisiting our personal legacies of growth and development can increase our awareness of those relational interactions that support our holistic development—and those that do not. Any idolizing of persons, positions, or practices almost always sets us up for serious troubles. When Father Leonard Feeney taught "There is no salvation outside the Church," he was in effect making an idol of an institution. This was bad practice! Bad practice too, is our idolizing familiar traditions and rituals; the kind that call for change. A favorite story about Dom Arrupe, the post-Vatican II leader of the Jesuits, tells of his clear, direct response to a burning change question. One of the priests attending the Jesuit conference asked: "Why do we no longer follow the time-honored rubrics for fasting, and other disciplinary observances?" Arrupe's answer: "Because we know more now." Yes, through inclusive studies, prayerful considerations, and amazing grace, we know more now. In our compassionate knowing, idols of belief and practice must be broken.

But we want our idols. And only the Truth can shatter them. Among the courageously committed scholars, the heroic writers of theological truth, Hans Kung stands tall. He, and others like him, have opened our eyes to the historical realities of the Bible, and have helped us change the way we see our "absolutes."

During the summer of 1968, I was at the University of Rhode Island enjoying a National Science Foundation grant to study microbiology. One morning before class, another participant handed me his morning newspaper, and motioned to the section he wanted me to read. The long report was on Pope Paul VI's encyclical, Humanae Vitae, which he promulgated in spite of expert advice that went firmly against it. The false idol of authoritarianism called Catholics to absolute obedience to a mandate which contradicted their mature consciences. Even to this day, insightful and sincere adults give little credence to such promulgations. Many ask: "Under what reasonable, humane rule or legislation would male celibate voices have the right to dictate how mature male and female adults live their intimate lives?"

It could be argued that the horrific human suffering of the Reformation and Counter-Reformation years were related to the systemic worship of idols: the Book versus the Church. Like other insidious diseases, ideological idolatry is not easily overcome. We today have no right to take on a condescending attitude towards the religious destructiveness of the Middle-Ages. Even when overwhelming evidence of pedophilia has been uncovered in USA, Ireland, Poland, and elsewhere, those within Catholic authority have hesitated, or refused to bring such heinous crimes against innocent children to justice. When the system is broken, the healing power of truth has work to do!

When teen-agers idolize popular performers, this is not the best practice. But, given adolescent identity issues, it is understandable. Unfortunately idol worship can easily be found among many adults. We find it not only among religious extremists, but also among the rank and file persons who disregard truth whenever their "idolatry" calls for it. This extremist attitude stifles normal psychological and spiritual development. It turns us away from any challenge of change, and keeps us prisoner to immaturity. Healthful growth and development allow for change. That is, there is no room for idols! Nor is there room for blame.

Among the irresponsible, the blame game is a favorite. The inability to live up to "idolized" ideals brings blame-throwers out of the woodwork. Scape-goating is not simply an Old Testament ritual. A neglected child grows up feeling insecure on many fronts. He or she enters adulthood with the habit of blaming others for their own perceived shortcomings. As destructive as blaming others can be, self-blame is even more problematic. Blaming ourselves for being "imperfect" keeps the irresponsible cycle going nowhere. Worst of all, this immaturity locks us in to a no-change lifestyle. We ask no questions of ourselves, of others, of institutions. We become know-nothing individuals who do-nothing, and wind up believing we are nothing. This makes for very poor psychospiritual health, and for a worthless change legacy.

The integration of psychology and spirituality supports holistic change, and is a legacy that encourages the creative growth process. Unquestioning acceptance of any kind of absolutism, whether religious or otherwise, is most emphatically not a good practice. No split between mind and feelings is welcome into the growing consciousness of healthy persons. In *The Heart of Philosophy*, Jacob Needleman makes several pithy comments, reminding us that ideas alone do not transform human life. We certainly need ideas, but we also need empowerment from another dimension of reality. Openness, readiness for the "other dimension," for the life force, comes through desire. It is in the struggle between attentions of the mind, and longings of the heart that a holy desire is born. Here we are faced with the discomfort—even pain—of awakening desire, of a change from managing our life, to transforming our life.

Needleman also underscores Socrates' admonition: "Give attention to the soul." Using different language, Jesus said the same thing. They both believed that we have within us something similar to the highest dynamic of the universe, the potential for transformative desire. Needleman's most elegant expression about the empowering quality of life's spiritual dimension assures us that "There is an all-pervasive Power and Mind outside of time and space which yet penetrates all time and space, penetrates downward into the human mind and the material world simultaneously, and which gives all orders of reality their structure and function. This is an aspect of a very ancient idea, lying at the root of every great spiritual teaching that the world has known."

One of my psychospiritual "learning points" about change came during a temporary summer job at a small suburban hospital where I filled in as a ward clerk. On a hot July afternoon, Mrs. D. was wheeled into a private room at the end of the fourth floor corridor. She was perfectly lucid. Her diagnosis: "inconclusive." After a week of consults by different specialists, each giving his own preferred prescription, Mrs. D. went "off the wall" with screaming, swearing, hitting, and fighting-mad reactions. Baffled, the experts withdrew all medications. Presto! Mrs. D. came back to her right senses. "If it ain't broke, don't fix it." And do not break it, so you have something to fix. This is not what real change is about!

Taking a close-up view of our change legacies may reveal our need to drop some of the mind-heart brokenness we have taken on from "experts," from authorities who "over-medicate" our minds with their "good advice"—which does little or nothing to advance our psychological and spiritual well-being, including a holy desire. When mandates of church, family, or group become burdensome, or worse, it might be time to change course, to let intuitive sense have its say. Staying connected to the essentials of our preferred spiritual tradition does not mean letting it take over depth of thought, or spontaneity of expression. It does mean giving up our fears and anxieties about change. It means opening our minds and hearts to a deeper consciousness of Reality, and trusting in life's Bigger Truth. Beyond the fears and anxieties of change, "The Spirit of Truth will guide you into everything that is true." (John 16:13)

Truth and Consequences

In his theological meditation about *The Church Maintained in Truth*, Hans Kung reminds us that we believers are maintained by God in truth wherever the Spirit is alive, guiding us into the way, and the life of authentic community. When Jesus promised that the Spirit of Truth would guide us into everything that is true (John 16:13), he was talking about a level of truth far beyond "facts." The Scriptures are not primarily interested in historical facts, but rather in that relevant truth which brings us beyond facts into well-being, "salvation," freedom.

Even as mature persons, we often find ourselves in an approach or avoidance relationship with truth. Our Western culture has primed us to prefer "the almighty fact," the absolute certainty of scientific data. We seem to have little or no patience with the ambiguity of symbols or myths which can, in themselves, hold the essence of God's truth. So we must help each other to give up our Linus blanket of absolutes, and live with whole-hearted confidence in the Spirit of Truth that will guide us.

If we can patiently meet the challenging discomforts of our fears and anxieties, then in due time, the truth will set us free to experience the fullness of life. Allowing God's truth to deeply influence our lives, and to ask as the prophet Samuel did, "Speak Lord, for your servant is listening." (1 Sam. 3:10) will guarantee grace-filled consequences.

Then there is the essential truth about death. Not death in the general sense, but our own particular death. Many of us believe that death is a transition from this life into Life that is far beyond any idea of an "afterwards" which we could possibly imagine. Personally, I do not expect to return to life as I now know it. I do expect to retain an identity in a different dimension.

In response to the Sadducees who did not believe in resurrection, Jesus pointed out to them that God told Moses: "I am the God of Abraham, of Isaac, of Jacob. God is not God of the dead but of the living." (Mark 12:26-27). Believing, and living in this resurrection mode calls us to make our own commitments to Life, and to experience the truth of God's vital presence, now!

For many of us, death is not so much the problem. Dying is! In *Credo*, Hans Kung wisely reflects, "Certainly human life is God's creation, but in accordance with the Creator's commission, it is also human responsibility." Consequently, both my living and my dying require personal determinations, unbiased reflections on God's truth.

Our right to a life and death worthy of our humanness also calls for the responsibility to seek respect and compassion for our final wishes. It is hard to find more significant issues than those wrapped around the life-to-Life concerns. Consequently, we look to the Spirit of truth to guide us in all that is true, especially as we make our decisions about how to live the truth each day of our lives.

And what does God's truth urge us to do? It reminds us to be always open to the challenges of change, to the truth that balance, flexibility, and compassion preempt our human preference for fixed rules and empty platitudes. God's truth reminds us that our struggle with anxiety and fear is a human happening that shifts with age and time, and that allows for our mistakes. It reminds us to be compassionately patient with ourselves so that we may readily relate to others in the same way.

God's truth reminds us that often the spontaneous desires of our hearts are valuable clues to the will of God for us. It reminds us to be aware of the movements of our hearts, to be sensitive to spiritual inspiration through the faithful practice of prayer and meditation. Without the practice of prayerful awareness, of interior quiet, we can hardly expect to experience the clarity, wisdom, and empowerment of God's truth.

A spiritually vibrant life supports and affirms our ability to "grow up," to think autonomously, to separate from "the group" in order to whole-heartedly follow the inspirations of the Holy Spirit. At the same time, we must be courageously aware of our human errors which sometimes present themselves as "holy insights." Prayer, meditation, and inspirational readings can help us stay keenly aware of the Truth, of life's spiritual dimension.

However, we must be careful to balance the theory of spirituality with its faithful practice. In *By Way of the Heart*, Wilkie Au makes this point by giving an appropriate quote from C.S. Lewis: "It is so fatally easy to confuse an aesthetic appreciation of the spiritual life with the life itself—to dream that you have waked, washed, and dressed, and then to find yourself still in bed."

In his trust in God's truth, Thomas Merton gave us a beautiful, prayerful, meditative moment. "My Lord God, I have no idea where I am going. I do not see the road ahead of me. I cannot know for certain where it will end. Nor do I really know myself, and the fact that I think that I am following your will does not mean that I am actually doing so. But I believe that the desire to please you does in fact please you. And I hope I have that desire in all that I am doing. And I know that if I do this you will lead me through the right road though I may know nothing about it. Therefore, I will trust you always though I may seem to be lost and in the shadow of death. I will not fear, for you are ever with me, and you will never leave me to face my perils alone." God's truth guides us always, and the consequences are blessings!

Reflective Moments

1. How is the balance between your need for both autonomy and inclusion given support by your family, and church community?
2. What are the wise discontents of your life? How do they keep you moving forward?
3. Why is it so necessary that you grieve for all the losses of your life, both great and small?
4. What might be several reasons for your acceptance of given precepts, and your hesitation to question traditional mandates?
5. When you take time to look inward, what spiritual growth needs might your discontents suggest? What symbols and myths of your spiritual heritage might be of value for you? Why?
6. How does "idolizing" persons, positions, or practices set you up for significant psychospiritual growth problems? How can you avoid these problems?

6.

ACCESS THE PSYCHOSPIRITUAL DIMENSIONS OF CHANGE

"New wine must go into new wineskins." (Mark 2:22)

Valuing Psychospiritual Change

When the human person meets the psychological and spiritual demands of change, expect sparks of friction to fly. For most of us "change" is a six-letter word of ill-repute! It can bring on adult temper tantrums, or even anxiety attacks. So why, in spite of the discomfort, do we still value change as an essential requirement for our personal and relational well-being? A very basic theory of change might read something like this: When healthful change choices are recognized and made, individuals can enjoy more satisfying relationships with self and others. Consequently, the communal rights of others are respected, judgmental and negative attitudes diminish, neurotic tendencies decrease, and comfort levels rise. So, when we accept the challenges of change, and make our own informed choices, these decisions move us forward toward psychological and spiritual enrichment, and a more enduring comfort zone.

Whether we readily accept it, or indignantly rage against it, change in our life is, like birth and death, an existential given. But this does not soften the fact that any kind of change can be a difficult life companion: not easy to live with, and impossible to live without! The improvement of most relationships, including our relationship with change, calls for a little finessing, and a skillful approach. Cognitive and intuitive insights are needed. For a start, we might reflect on the famous comedian, George Carlin's advice: "Ya gotta wanna!" As we saw in Jacob Needleman's advice, desire is essential.

Respectfully putting aside for a moment, the valuable scholarly findings of academic research, let us turn to our own experience. In today's high-tech culture where slowly paced, well-developed narratives take a back seat to the audio-visual blitz of endless surfing, of anti-literacy texting, of split-second movement, and of deafening noise, we find ourselves enveloped in this insane atmosphere. How can we possibly hold on to the essential relational art and skill of listening?

Listening is Janus-faced. It looks outward and inward at the same time. Outward attention, listening to others without inwardness, mimics Monkey Island, the Zoo's most popular tourist attraction. Like frenetic monkeys, our thoughts are all over the place, causing more confusion than comprehension. Attempts at listening to others, against the noise of our own fractured thoughts, gives a poor imitation of the art and skill of listening. Eye-to-eye contact is not enough. We need heart-to-heart contact, a listening that goes deeply into both thought and feeling, a listening that begins deeply within and then extends to others. A key question comes to mind: "Can we turn down the volume and activity of our Monkey-Island mind, and admit our need to listen deeply to our own fears and hesitations about change?

Listening inwardly to ourselves helps us listen outwardly to others. This kind of listening allows insights and healing to develop. It soothes troubled hearts; it makes life changes possible. If we are open to their message, dreams teach us a lot about ourselves, about how to listen to our deep inward needs. Jen shares one of her self-listening dreams. "Dusk sneaked in, wrapped itself around the day's fading shafts of light, and without apology, left me in a cold, unfamiliar place. Where was I? Signs along the winding, muddy roads spoke a foreign language. With chilling mists penetrating to the bone, with fatigue and hunger making misery acute, I would gladly give "my kingdom" for a cup of hot tea—and buttered cinnamon toast, too! But how did I get to this strange place? What was I doing here? No answers came. Instead, out of the night's blackness came two powerful horses, one black, one white, and both racing at breakneck speed directly towards me. Terrified, I gave out soundless screams. Abruptly, the mighty steeds stopped in their tracks, only inches from where I stood, frozen in fear. Lowering their noses, they gently nudged me in my side. Then without further incident, they disappeared as mysteriously as they came. In a cold sweat, amid muffled sobs, I woke up." Jen's dream would give Jungian analysts a field day, discussing symbolic meanings, and avenues of growth.

From a practical perspective, Jen's deep listening to her own inward narrative assures that she will probably hear and understand the message of her dream symbols. Inward listening touches the truth that what is natural is not to be feared. Change coming at us with the feel of a crushing stampede, may in the long run be a valuable learning experience. But we must be listening with an inner ear. In addition to dreams, our practice of prayerful reading, quiet meditation, private journaling, and confidential dialogue can also help to increase our effectiveness as good listeners.

Learning to listen deeply helps us to adjust and adapt to those experiences of change that keep us moving toward our highest psychospiritual potential. In our attempts to go with the flow of constructive change, we will face a key question: What do I want to gain, and what am I willing to give up? The choice of what to give up can be a very difficult decision. Yet, these let-go determinations must be our own. No advisor, seen or unseen, can call this shot. Only we as autonomous adults have the privilege and responsibility to discern what is in our own best interest. Others may offer informative facts and figures, but the buck stops with each of us. Either we make our well-considered choices for change, or we face the consequences of painful stagnation.

After months of inward listening and prayerful discernment, Louisa made her very difficult decision to terminate a long-standing relationship that was going nowhere. As it turned out, making the decision to disconnect was the easy part. Unexpected backlash in the form of feelings of unreality, nebulous fears, and emotional discomfort held her in knots for long torturous hours. Only when she took charge of herself by inward listening did she get relief. She told herself, "Whatever happens as a result of my decision, whether good or bad, I take full responsibility. And I trust in God's help as I make a new life for myself." In her up times and down times, Louisa remains grateful for having listened deeply to herself, for having made her own choice of change.

Instead of belonging only to specific growth stages, as certain developmental theorists suggest, change is an integral part of every age category: early, middle, and "senior." Our years of lived experience let us know whether change has been a life-enhancing factor for us, or whether sameness has been our stumbling block. During our introspective moments, honesty does not allow any excuses. We are faced with the privilege and responsibility of accepting those challenges of change which are uniquely ours, and which, when presented in our inward language, are for us alone to hear, understand, and act on.

Change is a worthy companion. It reminds us that as persons we are never "finished" but always "in process," always faced with the challenge "to become, or not to become." And when we are true to ourselves, true to our becoming, and when we are not always looking over our shoulders to get an okay sign from the party-line or the powers-that-be, then we can confidently, comfortably live with change.

You might argue that this is a glass half-full perspective. What about a more objective psychospiritual point of view? Turning again to John Bowlby and his study of the attachment and separation needs of children, he found that the abrupt change of losing the closeness of significant caregivers translated into a terrifying experience. This extreme relational change may not carry the same deadly fears for adults, but then again, in context, maybe it does. Brain imprints can be deeply enduring, gathering power over the years of lazy status quo attitudes.

Ageing does not offer immunity to the discomforts of change. But it does allow opportunities for critically examining any neurotic tendencies that rush in to fill our unmet developmental needs. In her study of the human personality, Karen Horney's *Self-Analysis*, uncovers the neurotic trends that stunt our growth. We all have legitimate needs for affection and approval, but when we find ourselves victim to approval ratings, to others' expectations, to dread of disagreements, we need change. When our center of gravity is outside our healthful psychospiritual identity, when we dread making demands or asserting our wishes, then we need change. Just as challenging are neurotic needs to control both ourselves and others through our idealizing intelligence and reason, through our dreading the realistic limitations of reason, and through the relentless drive for perfection. For each of us, at any point along the growth continuum, honesty and awareness of our conscious and unconscious driving forces must be acknowledged. Listening to our needs, accepting the challenge to change moves us toward personal and spiritual renewal. Buddha tells us that not to do this is like "one who looks up and spits at heaven; the spittle soils not the heaven, but comes back and defiles one's own person." In Mark 2:22, Jesus warns us that change is essential: "New wine must go into new wineskins." The message supporting change is clear! Will we accept it?

Healing Moments

1. Sit quietly, and slowly take several deep breaths.
2. Repeat softly, thoughtfully to yourself: "The spirit of Truth and Wisdom lives within me, and can help me to face the challenges of any kind of change.
3. Continue to breathe gently, and repeat your favorite "mantra" or brief prayer.
4. Focus on the life-force of the Higher Power that sustains us from moment to moment.
5. With compassionate affection, pray for yourself and for all creation, so that together we may be healed of our inner wounds, and be transformed in body, mind, and spirit.
6. Be joyful and thankful, and open yourself to the empowering Spirit of Change.

New Wine and New Wineskins

Early into his ministry, Jesus calls us to change. (Mark 1:15) Because his life's purpose was the fullness of our happiness and well-being, his urgings for change, although not always comfortable, were without exception, opportunities for blessings. As the advancing years enrich our lives with insights, courage, and wisdom, we often look for ways to transition from old familiar habits of thinking and acting to new, less familiar but more beneficial practices. Intentions to "change and believe" though sincere, are too often fragile and short-lived. Our determinations are easily over-ruled by old primitive brain imprints. Unless we keep the purpose, practice, and benefits of change front-and-center in mind and heart, our creative possibilities, and positive attitudes will quickly fade away.

How do we generate the wisdom and power to keep a positive attitude about life's necessary changes? Among our many options, shared narratives give us a fail-safe method. Our stories have power to enlighten, to encourage, and to heal. Jesus used them to great advantage throughout his earthly ministry. At the conclusion of his scholarly volume, *Jesus*, Eduard Schillebeekx recounts an incident told by Martin Buber: "A rabbi's grandfather was paralyzed. One day the old man was asked to tell something that happened with his teacher, the great Baalschem. Then he told how the saintly Baalschem used to leap about and dance while he was at his prayers. As he went on with the story, the grandfather stood up; he was so carried away that he had to show how the master had done it. From that moment on he was cured. That is how stories should be told." Incidentally, Schillebeeckx begins his book by repeating the healing story from Acts 4:10-12 where the lame man was cured when he heard from Peter, the story of Jesus.

When told honestly, respectfully, even reverently, our stories have great healing power. When we have ears to hear, when we listen attentively, the empowering message of the story gives new insight, and deeper meaning to our everyday happenings. Then, both narrator and listener find renewal and delight. Stories have great value for "children" of every age, from youngest to eldest. Stories help us to transition from primitive images of God to the more mature relationships with Ultimate Reality. Limited literal understandings of "the law" give way to a broader consciousness of expanding metaphors. Indeed, as Jesus taught, the new wine of creative, unconditional love can only be held in the new wineskins of changing human experience.

When Robert Coles was researching *The Spiritual Life of Children*, he found that across the broad spectrum of his interviews with children, the psychological picture of God can take almost any shape. God can be a friend or a potential enemy, a supportive admirer or a cynical critic, a source of encouragement or a reason for distress, anxiety, or despair. When the negative thoughts and feelings go without address, they cling to us, sucking life's vital energy, damaging the growing person, or worse, killing the person's potential for personal and spiritual advancement. By contrast, shared accounts of spiritual insights, of challenging experiences, of creative questions, all energize both the story-teller, and those who listen deeply.

One of my favorite story fragments, taken from a Robert Coles' spirituality interviews with children, relates to a young boy still in his first decade of life, watching a little squirrel chasing its tail—until it sees the boy. "Then it saw me . . . got an acorn . . . scurried up the tree and put it in the hole up there. I thought: I might be a big person, a god to that squirrel, and I reminded him that he should keep on track and not get caught wasting time. Maybe the Lord wants us to get down to business, like the squirrel did. We're here for something!" Yes, we are all here for something. Our shared stories help us to discern more clearly how that "something" is to be factored into the equation of our life.

If we take Jesus as our Model for being fully alive, we see clearly his easy comfort with self, his warm intimacy with God, his compassionate relationship with others. This is the same Jesus who valued stories, and used them to teach profound lessons to both simple and sophisticated listeners. What better example could we have? What better way of enriching ourselves and each other than by sharing the stories of our waking-up to God's presence within and beyond us, and to our need for change and growth.

Stories are the stuff our lives are made of, the tales that tell of our personal potential for creative expansion. Stories are the narratives that once shared, can generate energy, growth, and healing. No matter the age, interests, or cultural environment, listening to, and telling stories are universally accepted practices. The world's major religions all began with stories, many of which were eventually written and codified. Today, those who have a special interest in the unfolding of our spiritual consciousness often elicit fragments of stories by asking, "How do you picture God?" A five year old might answer, "He has long white whiskers, a big copybook where he writes himself notes about who is good and who is bad." A cynical adolescent's answer belies his irritability about the intrusive—and to him, irrelevant—question: "God is the almighty CEO, alone in his big sky office, his bare feet up on the desk, head tilted sideways against the big-back swivel chair, in a deep snoring sleep." A retiree in her late sixties has several different God stories: "Early on, God was absent to me; later, God became a curiosity; now God is the essence of my life."

Our shared stories form connections between and among minds and hearts that resonate with energy and information. This kind of connectedness generates an empowering sense of clarity, authenticity, and expanding consciousness. Through our heightened awareness, the Spirit of Life can more readily generate the new wine of creative ideas, and the new wineskins of meaningful change.

The Human Face of God

Like nature's pregnant seeds, stories hold great potential for change and healing. In revisiting the early years of my own childhood, a vivid memory of persistent curiosity about God finds easy access to instant recall. It is a story I enjoy sharing about a long-ago time, when with respectful determination, I put the query right out there: "What does God look like?"

The question was asked with the directness that only a child best knows. It was a cold, clear Sunday morning in the winter of a World War II year. Like most other necessities, gas was rationed, which meant that you had to use government coupons for purchasing certain things like shoes, butter, sugar, gasoline, and so forth. So I walked home from church with my parents and other car-less neighbors. Not long into our two-mile homeward hike, I put the question to my Dad: "Does God have a face?" He answered by giving my gloved hand a warm squeeze, and said nothing.

Grown-ups have a way of whispering their conversations which only attract little ears more certainly. My little "rabbit" ears were surely attracted to the conversation on the way home that morning. Mom was telling Mrs. Morris that my job was not only to pray for the safety of Uncle Albert who was among the soldiers headed for Anzio beach in Italy (a European war zone), but also for my friend's dad who was on a submarine warship somewhere in the Pacific (the Asian war zone). It seemed like every one of us was praying for all our soldiers and their families—even people we didn't know. Mrs. Morris said that she was so grateful to belong to a church that cares about everyone. "Imagine," she said, "praying together for all our neighbors, no matter what their religious beliefs." Mr. Morris' tummy started to shake as he laughed out loud. He said something about Mark Twain, but I couldn't understand what he meant.

Being a persistent kid, when we got home I again pushed my Dad for an answer. And he pushed me to find the answer for myself. He said softly, "You saw the face of God this morning." I knew even at the age of six that when Dad answered with a riddle, it was his way of saying that he expected me to figure the answer out for myself. I walked away, impatient for the day when I would know as much as he did.

Now, many decades later, gas is "stamp free" and I ride comfortably to and from church on any day that I wish to join a communal worship ritual. And on occasion, I do not hesitate to share my worship time with friends of different religious persuasions. Over these past decades, I have learned to accept (reluctantly, at times) necessary changes in perspective, along with the wisdom it brings. I can also appreciate more deeply my Dad's refusal to give a direct answer to my Face of God question. The ageing process has taught me that the truly important questions have many and different answers, and the answers are often less important than the questions.

Does God have a face? With all due respect for the hermeneutic expertise of Biblical scholars, and for the academic knowledge of theologians, I prefer to define Face as an "expression, semblance, showing" of God among us. I have been assured by reputable sources that the concept of Church means primarily the "people of God." Would it not make good sense then to find the semblance of God among the people within a caring community, within a loving Church?

In these days of technological wizardry and ever expanding data banks, one reads and hears much about racism, sexism, and ageism. The words themselves so easily elicit negative connotations. And what about churchism! Does it also signal myopia, exclusiveness, rigidity, power-over, and refusal to change and grow? Where is the mutuality, the freedom that celebrates ecumenism, that celebrates the value of various religious traditions, that celebrates the creative power of change?

If churchism exists among us with its narrow parochial mind-set, and its refusal to respect the authentic religious traditions of other Christians and non-Christians, then perhaps the Face of God remains hidden, humanly speaking. If on the other hand, we become more open to change and to sharing our spiritual growth narratives, then we can create opportunities for seeing God's "face."

As Eduard Schillebeeckx so well put it, "All Christians must strive for a unity, the model for which does not fully exist in any single church. Unity is future for all the Christian churches, not a return to any old situation." The suggestion is not that we lose our particular perspectives and preferred traditions, but that we reflect the Godliness of our spiritual identities through an inclusiveness which brings authentic well-being to body, mind, and spirit. And that shows God's "face." But when will we open ourselves more fully to each other in the Spirit of inclusive love? Perhaps when we learn to listen more compassionately to each other's stories of challenge, change, and spiritual renewal, we will then find courage to share our own personal narratives about experiencing God's presence.

Healing Moments

1. Sit quietly, and breathe gently for several seconds.
2. Focus on your familiar responses when any change experience faces you.

3. Remind yourself that feelings of discomfort about change, transition, and loss are very normal. We all have our own unique responses that are not necessarily good or bad.
4. Encourage yourself to understand and accept your experiences of change challenge, no matter when, where, how, or why they come.
5. Consider practical ways you can more consistently expand your psychological and spiritual consciousness. Ask yourself relevant questions.
6. Admit the real challenge of this "interior work" and trust in that Higher Power that helps you to know and appreciate the blessings of change.

Discernment and Change-Ability

Before we look more closely at spirituality in the context of change, let us remember that any dualistic way of thinking about our human experiences is incompatible with truth. This includes the way we think about spirituality. To support dualism as a way of comprehending the human condition, leads to ignorance. A basic fact about the human person cannot be denied: The integration of body, mind, and spirit form a unified mode of being. On this note, Jung cautions that "we must reconcile ourselves to the mysterious truth that the spirit is the life of the body seen from within, and the body is the outward manifestation of the life of the spirit—the two being really one."

When we consider the holistic nature of humanity, we can appreciate that as we come to "know more," to grow more, our religious perspectives must be in constant scrutiny, revision, and verification. Psychologically and spiritually we continue to create ourselves through change and growth opportunities. In general terms, when we consider the practical relationship between spirituality and everyday living, we are talking about concern for others' well-being, as well as for our own growth and transformation. We cannot give what we do not have! In other words, unless we are open to change and holistic transformation, the empowerment that fosters personal and spiritual well-being will not be ours to share. In *Ethics for the New Millennium*, the Dalai Lama points out that "Due to the fundamental interconnectedness which lies at the heart of reality, your interest is also my interest. From this it becomes clear that "my" interest and "your" interest are intimately connected."

In our understanding and practice of spirituality, it is awareness that enables us to change, to move forward toward personal transcendence. Awareness, not of idealistic goals, but as Meister Eckhart tells us, awareness of "that which, in God, we have always been." When we live each moment in awareness, eventually little "enlightenments" will be ours. Gradually, we will let go of ideals that keep us tied to childish fears, and to our own neurotic tendency toward "perfection." Purposeful change brings freedom from self-aggrandizement and egocentric "morality." In *The Silence of Unknowing*, Terrance Grant sums up our need for awareness. "We need only allow the Spirit to enlighten us, to help us see why we really do the things we do—however praiseworthy they may seem to be on the surface. Then we will have within us the liberating grace of awareness." This self-knowledge, this self-awareness serves as a significant step toward experiencing God in ordinary life. And this is what it means to live our spirituality.

Psychological and spiritual awareness of our self and of our connection with others—even with the universe—brings us to the practice of inward prayer. This is not about words, petitions, confessions, etc. This kind of prayer focuses primarily on presence, on our presence and the Divine Presence. Because there are no long lists of rules, directives, and theories for this type of prayer, it often feels nebulous or vague. Some describe it as "difficult," or "mystic." Most attempts to describe prayer of the heart fall far short of its reality. In his essay on prayer, Thomas Merton tells us: "Prayer of the heart introduces us into deep interior silence so that we learn to experience its power. For that reason, prayer of the heart has to be always simple, confined to the simplicity of acts, and often making use of no words and no thoughts at all." Merton goes on to caution us about using too many words, especially when words are no longer useful. He also warns us against our "stubbornly insisting upon compulsive routines which seem to us to be necessary because they accord with our short-sighted notions." The holy among us, including Merton and mystics from any of the world's major religions, believe that our spiritual practices have no point, no purpose if they are not firmly rooted in this life, in openness to others, in love for others.

Along with awareness, the practice of discernment readies us for productive, purposeful change as we journey "from law to love." In her *Spirituality and Personal Maturity*, J.W. Conn mentions Christian discernment as being the Spirit's gentle guidance which "is possible only through an examination of the inner psychological states that motivate and permeate action." She goes on to say, "discernment requires self-directed judgments based on critical self-knowledge and the ability to trust and evaluate our experience of God; otherwise, it is compulsion, conformity to external authority, or reading tea leaves." The point is clear: keen awareness and honest discernment are foundational factors at every step of our life's personal, spiritual journey.

Like every good teacher, Jesus asked a lot of questions. In John 1:38, he wants to know: "What are you looking for?" He wanted his disciples to be clear on what they desired, on what they really wanted of life. It is not difficult to imagine his follow-up question: "What changes of mind and heart will you set in motion to achieve your goal?" This challenge turns many of his followers away sad. A chronic weakness among those of us who want more of life is this: We tend to use our favorite excuses and strategies against growth change. We find ingenious ways to defend ourselves against any ideas or actions that might challenge our "ideals," our "idols." To bring desired change we need clarity, determination—and discernment.

The practice of prayerful discernment can help us decide more definitively what we want and how we might move forward. Discernment clarifies the integral connection between who we are, and who we are called to be. Discernment opens us to a more inclusive reflection on life's pragmatic events, on personal cognition and feelings, on the silent touch of God's faithful presence. While ordinary discernment has its practical advantages, spiritual discernment affects deeper, far reaching possibilities for change and renewal.

By now the reader knows that my approach to personal change and spiritual renewal is holistic. That is, we are all integrated body, mind, and spirit persons who are connected to each other, to the Universe, to God. From this perspective, discernment takes on its holistic identity. It calls us to persist in our struggle to be loving persons, to be open to change, to trust in a Higher Power. It calls us to question rigid rules and rituals, and to remember that growth is on-going. It calls us to allow for trial and error experiences, some of which may be very painful. It calls us to on-going conversion through creative change in our thoughts, attitudes, feelings, values, and behaviors.

It is interesting to note that our spontaneous desires are valuable clues to the "will of God" for us. Merton reminds us that if we are afraid of spontaneity, it might be because we have a warped idea that spontaneity is "merely natural," that for things to be supernatural, they must cause us pain and frustration. He assures us that the truth is quite different. If our discernment is going to be effective, we must be aware of the data of our heart. Reason and emotion, head and heart, are both critical components of holistic decision making. After a period of testing, of positive feelings like hope, peace, joy, and confidence that persists, then we can be reasonably assured that the decision or choice that we made was the right one.

The following discernment outline is based on the *Spiritual Exercised*, by Ignatius of Loyola:

1. Focus your concern on to your mental "radar screen."
    . How alert, rested, and informed am I?
    . What must I do to help myself become more focused?
2. Focus on your "bottom line" purpose in life.
    . How free am I from inordinate attachments?
    . In what ways can I help myself become more balanced?
3. Focus on examining the particular concern more thoroughly.
    . How have I allowed silence and prayer to guide my considerations?

. Have I engaged self-knowledge, cognition, and intuition in this process?
4. Focus on the advantages and disadvantages of resolving this concern.
. In what ways would my life be enriched by resolving this concern?
. What are the possible disadvantages or discomforts involved?
5. Focus on your readiness to make a decision.
. In what ways do head and heart signal toward a decision?
. What do my honest, holistic reflections suggest?
6. Focus on the ultimate purpose of the unique life that is yours.
. How do I manifest an honest appreciation of myself?
. Can I live peacefully and productively with my change decision?

The practice of discernment helps us live our spirituality with purpose and integrity. It reminds us to confront issues, think about the consequences of our decisions, and then make the necessary changes. Discernment has us following Jesus' habit of asking catalytic questions that give us a wake-up call to maturity, and rejects any idea of God that would keep us infantile. The discernment process must take into account our total personal sensing of a situation. It must open us more fully to life. Through the practice of discernment we learn to give up our most cherished images of ourselves and to adjust to reality. We learn that grace is not a substitute for nature; theology is not a substitute for concrete evidence.

Again, a cautionary note: Because awareness and discernment are such an integral part of our psychospiritual development, we are well-advised to be careful in our analysis and conclusions about growth and change. Simplifications of developmental complexities may help to clarify theories and practices, but simplifications can also distort. In his *By Way of the Heart*, Wilkie Au warns us: "The history of thought contains many examples of how complex realities can suffer from over-simplification or distortive reductionism."

Complexities of real life discernment issues face Karen, a middle-age teacher of Church history at a private, progressive college. She, her husband, and their twelve-year-old daughter have been loyal members of a fundamentalist Christian church for several years. Karen, an informed, talented teacher has accepted her husband's "old school" religious preferences in order to avoid his temper outbursts. Since intelligent discussion of their different needs proved impossible, "acceptance" has been Karen's way of keeping "peace."

However, now that her daughter is asking the wake-up, shake-up queries that gifted adolescents love to ask, Karen is second-guessing her resolve. Circumstances have changed, and her concern is now for her daughter's psychological and spiritual development. Karen is not looking for "left wing permissiveness," but neither can she accept "right wing rigidity." Her daughter deserves to be free from a condescending, patriarchal, top-down church organization that mandates behaviors belittling to women. Karen is prayerfully discerning her options. In her place, what would you choose?

Whatever Karen's choice will be, it must reflect her prayerful study and thoughtful consideration of essential developmental changes. Manipulative mandates fail to adequately respect the Spirit living in us, the Spirit calling each of us to taste fully God's truth, freedom, and joy. To be growing psychospiritually means to be learning always. According to Thomas Merton, we are always beginners, always capable of expanding our possibilities for learning and loving. In his *The Way of Chuang Tzu*, he reminds us that clinging to one partial view, to one limited opinion, and to treat this as "the answer" is to dishonor God, ourselves, and each other. Today, spirituality reaches out beyond the known and into the systemic realization that every unique individual remains a significant part of God's unifying and dynamic Whole. In the final analysis, this means that our day-to-day awareness of God's real presence in our lives is what our psychological and spiritual well-being is really all about.

In the epilogue of his *Great Christian Thinkers*, Hans Kung hopes for a relevant post-modern theology that holds "truthfulness as a thoughtful account of faith which investigates and speaks the Christian truth." Expanding personal consciousness, broadening cognitive and intuitive awareness of the truth, establishes a solid base for personal, spiritual development, no matter what faith tradition one follows. Half-truths confuse, discourage, and under mind any honest attempt to live in the Truth.

For herself and her daughter, Karen wants truthfulness, along with an ecumenism that shows an enlightened appreciation for the different paths to Truth. Ecumenism supports personal uniqueness within every community. It also encourages dialogue with those communities outside the Judeo-Christian traditions. Perhaps ecumenism's greatest value lies in its call for mutual respect, and the sharing of insights, experiences, and questions related to Ultimate Reality.

Karen looks for at least one other psychospiritual quality of life, especially for her young daughter: liberation. Without apology, liberation scrutinizes images of God that depict a controlling, punishing, patriarchal power whose subjects live in chronic fear, guilt, and insecurity. Well-conceived rules can be helpful, but we must be mindful of their limited value. Because they are fallible indicators, they should be used prudently, even sparingly—as was Jesus' practice.

Karen, like many loving Christian parents, will find the courage to follow discernment's choice. In and through his life, Jesus exemplified courage at every turn of events, including those situations when he stood against his own people who showed exclusive action against "unclean," "disreputable," "different" individuals or groups. As the Scriptural historian, John P. Meier describes Jesus, he was a courageous marginal Jew. Courage is needed if we are to follow in his "marginal" footsteps, if we are to love God with all our heart, with all our soul, with all our mind, and with all our strength, and our neighbor as our self. (Mark 12:28-34) This is, of course, very difficult—but not impossible. "With God, all things are possible." (Matthew 19:26) Karen has good reason to rejoice! Our ability to change, to imagine more meaningful ways of being and doing, mark us as one of Nature's most significant achievements.

The memory is still vivid. Genetics laboratory investigations ran all morning. Even when the air-conditioner droned at full blast, the August humidity seeped into our space and the signature odors of formaldehyde, and other chemical smells hung heavy in the air. We fifteen undergraduate biology majors readied our lab stations for the preliminary, simple work of identifying the chromosomes of a mosquito larva. The procedures were clear and straight forward. But not one of us could find the stained chromosomes. A dozen or more tries, and still nothing! Excellent laboratory technique was one of my strong points, so why did this no-brainer procedure keep coming up empty of results? Finally, flexibility and a willingness to change the accepted technique saved the hour. My questions kept coming: Might the blotting step need some adjustment? Might the procedural directives lack nuance? Given the quality of the supplies we were using, might there be a need to move beyond the "absolutes" of accepted custom, and change to a more gentle technique for the absorption procedure? Right on! Switching to a very light blotting technique did the trick. Finally, my larva's chromosomes showed clearly on the 'scope's high-power field. My lesson learned that morning had little to do with genetics, and much to do with the value of keeping a flexible mindset, one that does not hesitate to question the "rules," and then confidently change directions as needed.

The practical benefits of change-ability speak for themselves. The spiritual advantages may not always be so obvious. In Mark 7:1-13, we find Jesus exposing the danger of narrow-minded, rigid traditions. Although at no point was Jesus ready to dispense willy-nilly with the real message of God's love laws, he was always ready to be compassionately flexible where personal and spiritual well-being were concerned.

When reflecting on the benefits of change-ability, most of us have our favorite stories. One inspiring example of a courageous "David" standing against a powerful "Goliath" encourages my own determination to see beyond the rules, and to resist blind conformity. The example comes from a segment of Therese Martin's life, given by Jean Guitton in his book, *The Spiritual Genius of Saint Therese of Lisieux*. Therese repeatedly takes us back to the Gospel mandate of Jesus, and refuses to be impressed or intimidated by pompous or counterfeit imitations of his message.

One of my favorite stories about Therese finds her asking Pope Leo XIII for permission to become a Carmelite nun, even though she was not quite sixteen years old, the minimal age requirement for acceptance into the community. Therese, not satisfied with the Pope's nebulous response, insists that just one word from him could solve her whole problem. When fifteen year old Therese gives indication that she intended to further argue her case, the two papal guards, and the priest-guide remove her from the scene. She was not then, or ever after, over-awed by title or circumstance. Therese knew the rules well, yet her autonomy allowed her to see their limitations, to appreciate contextual necessity, to courageously stand her ground. And she did have her way.

Every personal narrative must be seen in the context of its historical and cultural milieu. Therese was born in 1873, and died in 1897 at the young age of twenty-four. Guitton tells us that her spontaneity, assurance, and determination helped to make her the unusual person she was "in her particular time and place." Therese would probably add: "Yes, grace does such things."

Another favorite example from within my own denominational tradition is Francis DeSales, a sixteenth century noble gentleman. During the "fighting mad" and hateful years of the Reformation and Counter-Reformation, Francis was a refreshing change from the leadership style on both sides of the great theological divide. DeSales was remarkable for his respectful, warm manner, and his lack of ostentation or pomposity. In his diocese of Savoyard, he cared for his peasants, showed compassion to all. He proved his belief to be true: We accomplish more through love and charity than through severity and rigor. In a time of changeless "absolutes" DeSales made clear his conviction that every person, clergy or lay, male or female is capable of finding an appropriate way to God. His example of psychological and spiritual autonomy still resonates for us today.

Matteo Ricci, another sixteenth century psychospiritual giant, dialogued with Confusian scholars during his missionary work in China. Yes, Ricci converted any number of Chinese to Christianity. But his connection with Confusion wisdom also "converted" Ricci. The end result was a mutual understanding and respect that flourished between what were previously antagonistic approaches to Reality. European custom of his time, mandated that Ricci maintain rigid conformity to Western dress and protocol. After his respectful dialogue with Confusion scholars, after he learned and appreciated their thoughts and cultural legacy, Ricci changed his dress, grew his beard, and adopted their lifestyle. More significantly, he also changed his thinking and his attitudes. Although he still found much to criticize in superstition, and in oppressive social order, Ricci was able to find God working in the lives of his non-Christian friends. Because he could maintain an open attitude and respectful converse, Ricci's change-ability brought the Christian message to a foreign culture.

On a personal note, why after so many years do I still stay connected—through prayer and reading—with these examples of what I call "holy change-ability?" Why do I respectfully consider their sometimes disturbing questions, insights, and experiences? Why do I deliberately choose to reflect deeply on their transformative examples? Because the paradigm of change holds true: New times bring new circumstances, bring new perspectives, bring new choices, and bring new opportunities for renewal and transformation.

The Healing Power of Presence

Change of any kind can be counted on to leave wounds of real consequence. In body, mind, and spirit, we experience varying degrees of pain or discomfort whenever change, transition, and loss touch our lives. Beyond the usual ways of comforting and supporting each other in times of need, what can be done? How might we transmute the wounds of change into the blessings of healing?

Courageously admitting our pain and confusion is a good start. In realizing that our brokenness, our vulnerability, can open us to God's healing power, gives us some comfort. Yes, we want to be healed so that we can more effectively help others to heal. On this point Henri Nouwen reminds us that we are all wounded healers. We are all in need of compassionate care.

Many of the life changes that we experience leave wounds that call for our healing of body, mind, and spirit. When we suffer from debilitating headaches, allergies, asthma, arthritis, or chronic illnesses, we need holistic healing. When we feel disempowered by fear, anxiety, anger, or confusion, and when we are periodically overcome by distrust, or depression, our need for healing is clear. Sometimes in addition to the wounds of physical and psychological changes, we face our own spiritual neediness, our inability to forgive ourselves or others. When this happens, we are truly in need of deep healing. The prayerful, mindful approach to well-being is not a substitute for other practical, action-centered methods of meeting our needs. However, there is real healing power in every authentic, compassionate presence. And this empowering presence deserves fair acknowledgement.

To be authentically present to ourselves and to others involves being deeply, comfortably conscious of life's spiritual dimension. This kind of awareness establishes a loving presence of person to person. Being fully present in this way fosters support, healing, and renewal. We can share this holy presence in various ways: during momentary reflections, at times of communal worship, or in deliberately chosen moments when we focus on a loved one.

In order to be fully, mindfully present to each other, we must first be keenly aware of our own essential being, of that vital, empowering Force within us. Awareness of this reality lends healing power to intrapersonal connection with self, and to interpersonal relations with others. In effect, this expanded consciousness allows the Holy Spirit (or Ultimate Reality, if you prefer) to channel healing power through our human presence.

Spiritual growth, and healing of our change-wounds are experiences not easily measured. But it is probably safe to conclude that our loving presence does, in fact, advance the holistic well-being of those who choose to connect with each other through an expanded awareness, and through acts of compassionate caring.

And for those who doubt the legitimacy and power of being fully presence, or who hesitate to open their minds and hearts to a broader, creative perspective, why not invest in a copy of *Why God Won't Go Away*, by Andrew Newberg, M.D.! He will remind you that the new discipline of neurotheology takes a close look at what it means to be spiritually present. You will find that as long as we humans have minds and hearts capable of sensing the reality of the Divine Presence, spiritual empowerment and real healing will happen.

When we attend closely to Jesus' message, we find his description of Divine indwelling as more than a simple image of God. It is the very presence of God. It is this Holy Spirit within us that enables us to know, and love each other. We are given a new mandate to love in concrete, compassionate ways. (John 13:34) It is this empowering presence of the Spirit that can transform, and heal us. In *The World's Religions*, Huston Smith uses the example of energy locked within the center of the atom, as a reminder of the power we each carry locked within our hearts. This locked-in power to heal ourselves and others is nothing more or less than God's own love, alive in us. This empowering love does not usually do its healing work through clever conversation, front-page heroism, or other acknowledgements of "good deeds." Healing work is often done in small, hidden, ordinary, even unexpected ways.

Nan was a college freshman, who with her upperclassman date attended his friend's family celebration: an upscale, Philadelphia, Main Line engagement party. Since she was not a Main Liner, Nan knew only a few of the college-set guests and no one among the family, or other adult invitees. By an unexpected turn of events, she suddenly found herself lost within an unfamiliar group of visitors. As soon as the host of the party realized Nan's predicament, he quietly led her back to the gathering of her college friends, and with the greatest of gentle concern and sensitivity, made sure that she was once again comfortable with her own age group. He made her feel a valued and most welcome part of this family's celebration. Although she initially felt like an "outsider" at this party, the authentic respect and loving attention she received from the host and other family members, empowered Nan to believe in her own valued presence. Here among these strangers she felt the warm acceptance that spoke without words.

Nan said that she still carries with her the memory of that unexpected experience of a holy presence, of comforting empowerment that seemed to invisibly radiate from this kind, and caring family. "Who you are speaks so loudly, I can't hear what you are saying." Nor did they need to say much. Their presence fulfilled the mandate of Francis of Assisi: "Go preach the Gospel; use words only if you have to." Compassionate presence has healing power!

Reflective Moments

1. What challenging obstacles did you (or do you) encounter in your efforts to understand and heal your wounds of change?
2. To what extent have you considered the value of "ordinary" persons who model the great virtues, as compared to the hagiographic accounts of "saintly" lives? How do you discern the difference?
3. Seeing change as a valuable companion helps us to value our "in process" human condition. How are you dealing with the attachment and separation challenges that change presents?
4. Our shared stories can help us to explore new ways of thinking. What part of your own life's journey might help you appreciate the challenge and blessing of change?
5. How could your understanding and practice of spirituality be enhanced by your awareness of the value of change?
6. Our spiritual growth and the healing of change-wounds are not easily measured. Nevertheless, how can you further the empowering work of the Holy Spirit within yourself and others?

7.

BEGIN HOLISTIC RENEWAL NOW

"You must have salt in yourselves, and live at peace with each other." (Mark 9:50)

Meeting the Demands of Change

If W.H. Auden is correct when he suggests "We would rather be ruined than change," then we have lots of work to do! Unless we meet the demands of change, we can indeed be ruined. At any age, young or old, the necessities of making life adjustments by moving in a new direction, by letting go of familiar comforts (or even discomforts) all require a firm, even heroic determination. But habits, long in the making, are not easily changed. Habits of control can be as harmfully addictive as alcohol, tobacco, caffeine, or any of the hard-core drugs available on the market. Habits of control often give the illusion that we are secure, invulnerable, and beyond the change demands of real life. These are of course flights of fancy, poor pretensions at being in control.

Our control habits might be categorized in simple terms as either productive or destructive. When we take control of our choices, of those determinations that responsibility lays at our feet, life enhancing changes for ourselves and others can result. Choosing to develop healthful nutritional habits instead of pigging-out on junk foods obviously holds both short and long term advantages. But on the other hand, when supermarket shopping carts get filled each week with processed foods and high fructose "goodies," then these bad "control" habits can do us in. Why would anyone choose a dead-end path to diabetes? "No one is going to tell me how to live my life!" Here we have a classic comment that carries hidden truth, except when made by a "control idiot." Without the right kinds of control, dysfunctional habits can lead directly to ruin. Ignoring frontal lobe brain directives, while following primitive brain inclinations, can prevent productive change.

Productive change can only do its good work of enhancing our holistic health and general well-being when we think and act rightly, when we choose to live by those constructive habits that meet the demands of change. And if we don't? "There ain't no free lunches!" The price for making bad choices and for having destructive habits of imagined control must be paid. The price? Psychospiritual dis-ease!

Productive habits of control enhance our life experiences. They reflect self-understanding and compassionate concern for self and others, even as they sensitively support necessary life changes. Emily and Jack faced their own kind of change "demands." Determined as they were to be no burden for their grown children, this couple had to flesh out an acceptable retirement plan. After months of research, they were finally ready to make an informed but difficult decision: a move to a continuing care retirement community. Like our four-legged house pets, "seniors" do not abandon old habits easily. No matter how attractive the idea of retirement living may be, the distasteful work of packing "stuff," ridding the basement of "good junk," planning the moving strategies, all demand a positive perspective, a deliberate choice for significant change. Productive habits of control allow us to change what we can, to accept what we cannot, and to know the difference. But even our well-planned choices for change do not come easily. The letting go part is always a huge challenge.

If letting go is the singularly great, difficult demand of change, why are we so ill-prepared to "let go," to move ahead? We each have our own favorite answer to the reason for our clinging to dysfunctional habits. But I like Neil Armstrong's reason for accepting the change mentality. At age ninety-two, this former astronaut told his interviewer that at NASA they were always "trained for everything that might go wrong." In effect, they simply could not hang on to favorite perspectives or procedures. Readiness for creative change had to become a taken-for-granted habit, a way of life. Unfortunately few of us are encouraged to develop the habit of letting go, even when necessity calls for "a different way." Not only are we not prepared to change course, we hardly imagine, or take time to consider that changing circumstances might demand a change in plan.

Some might argue that change is going on all the time. Look at the technological explosion. Postmodern life seems to be a perpetual change experience. This, of course, is true, but too generalized a view. We are well aware of the deadly effects that uncontrolled, fast cellular changes cause to the human body, or that uncontrolled, fast conceptual changes cause to the human mind. Cancer and schizophrenia are definitely not productive changes. Preparedness for a controlled productive change does not call for an overload of "stuff," no matter its value. Rather it calls for a wise letting go habit.

Simply talking about "letting go" has its value. But how do we go about the doing of it? A few practical suggestions are offered here, to encourage thoughtful discourse and courageous action. For starters, acknowledge those persons, places, things that hold you attached. Attachments of any kind usually form a network of connections that include exclusive preferences. These, in turn, have the feel of possessiveness. Not only objects, but ideas also have a stick-to feel. For example, are we ready to let go of condescending attitudes about certain religious mandates, biblical perspectives, or "foreign" customs? Are those of us who are Christians, ready to follow Jesus' habit of letting go of family ties, of traditional protocol, of condemnatory rules?

Staying with Jesus' example (or even Socrates', or Buddha's), letting go is not an end in itself. Nature abhors a vacuum. Can we fill the letting go space as Jesus did with concern and compassion? This brings us to a core issue of change, one that goes beyond "outer concerns" to our "inner concerns." Our letting go habits allow needed space for inward growth. Our letting go habits invite opportunities for personal and spiritual renewal, and take us into the very heart of productive change.

Our letting go habits open us to the empowerment of grace that brings self-understanding, and self-acceptance. This positive attitude helps to generate compassionate communal living. A close, meditative consideration of our Model's own game plan for his followers is enlightening: "You must have salt in yourselves, and live at peace with each other." (Mark 9:50)

Jesus gave us the challenge. We must make our own choices. Every major world religion has its favorite saints. And down through the centuries many of us have our own chosen, favorite few who have helped us to have salt in ourselves, and to live at peace with each other. I have already mentioned my favorites, in order to spark your interest in finding your own meaningful models. However, closer scrutiny of contemporary circumstances has opened me to unexpected postmodern models who have modified, changed, or enriched my perspective on the "good news."

Having grown up with a Catholic, pre-Vatican world view, I carry my own brand of wounds and scars of change. Most of us already know that in healthy, fully functioning persons the body, mind, and spirit work in harmonious synchronicity. We also know that this harmony is dynamic—not static. Characteristic of all flourishing life is this vigorous, receptive, alive quality. To be unchanging is to be dead! Jesus, and other supporters of human flourishing, call us to fullness of life, to metanoia, to essential and on-going developmental change.

When I was growing up "holy" in the pre-Vatican II generation, there were no doubts about what was right or wrong, acceptable or unacceptable, true or false. Concerns about change or uncertainty never stirred the still waters of our complacency. Patriarchal church authority had set things straight once and for all. "per omnia saecula saeculorum." Life was not always easy, but it was always unambiguous, clear, and certain. And for most of us, not yet grown-ups, it was all quite comfortable—until change blew in with its challenging new perspectives, audacious questions, and bold aggiornamento.

To take the challenges of change seriously, we need to think and act in relevant ways. We need to see our lives from an expanded, meaningful perspective. We need to awaken a desire for an authentic way of life, for one that includes a vision of who I am behind the appearance I give. The call to transformative change is an invitation to wholeness, to a broader vision of what constitutes holistic health, or if you prefer, "sanctity."

Along with those who try to take seriously the call to meaningful change, I have made a paradigmatic shift in how I envision holiness. The psychospiritual models of today who closely resemble Jesus' way, are not necessarily world-famous. Rather, they are more often the "hidden ones" whose lives are simple, compassionate, and hardly front-page news. For example, a few weeks ago I accidentally made a wrong turn while driving home from an afternoon appointment. Ordinarily a driver will easily rectify her mistake, and be on her merry way—in the right direction. Not so, if like me, the driver is dyslexic, and has no sense of direction. After driving at least twenty miles (in the wrong direction) I pulled into a gas station, went to the back of the store, and asked two workers for help. Perhaps they read the panic in my face, and felt compassion for my out-of-town confusion. With great patience and clarity they wrote out the easiest, most direct way for me to get back on track. I have no idea who they are, but for their spontaneous, generous help during a hectic, high volume work day, I will always be grateful. And I will always be challenged to be as compassionate to others as they were to me.

Less personal examples are also a part of my "hidden saints" list. Many of my friends are in pastoral ministry. They are rarely, if ever, not on call. Even on a day-off, the phone can signal an emergency that has them back on call at a moment's notice. And what about dedicated parents, teachers, physicians, police, firemen, military personnel! The list of dedicated models seems endless. The "miracles" they perform do not hit the headlines. Except every once in a while! Journalist Steve Lopez shares his "miracle" experience of Nathaniel Anthony Ayers in his book titled, *Soloist*, the comeback story of a mentally challenged musical genius. Lopez's true story has all the ingredients of a metanoia experience: change, compassion, challenge, choice, and transformation. Let us be reminded: holistic renewal is where we find it; it is all around us everywhere.

Back to an essential! Learning to let go opens us to the personal and spiritual renewal that is possible when we allow transformative change to have its way. Across the globe chaos seems to reign. Yet even in the chaos, pockets of "believers" learn to let go of their exclusive ways of thinking and acting, and they begin to embrace a compassionate inclusive attitude. In their contemporary circumstances, in their inimitable way, ordinary saints of today are meeting the demands of change. They are showing us what it means to be the "salt of the earth."

Habits of Renewal

Whether from hearsay, reading, or life experience most of us will agree that "first we form our habits, and then our habits form us." The word "habit" holds profound meaning for those with open hearts and discerning minds. In *The Will to Meaning*, Viktor Frankl reminds us: "It is a prerogative of being human, and a constituent of human existence, to be capable of shaping and reshaping oneself." If we see ourselves as victims of circumstances and their influences, we insult our human dignity and diminish our determination to change. Yes, we make our habits; we can also break their hold on us. We need not become victims of our own habits.

Don and his friend Al picked me up on a cold November evening. Off we went, bouncing along in his Jeep for the three mile run to a spacious, but packed room at a church meeting hall. The AA meeting began promptly. When new members were asked to raise their hands, Don leaned over and whispered to me, "Jeez! I made a mistake. The meeting for visitors is next week—not tonight!" And so I was welcomed as a new member. At the half-way, refreshment break, several confirmed members came to personally welcome me. First came a young scrawny, black-toothed, multiple addiction woman who encouraged me to stay with the program. Then there was a handsome, business-suited, middle-aged man who shook my hand and commended me for deciding to join AA. Before the break ended, a poorly dressed "bag lady" gave me assurance that everyone there was pulling for me, and that I must not give up on myself. When the break ended, the main speaker of the evening began. In sharing his long journey from his addiction habit, to his near-death experience, to his final recovery, he told a tale of challenge, defeat, denial, desperation, and renewal. Segments of his journey to-and-from the brink of death remain filed in my memory bank under "do not forget."

As a chemist for a nationally known chemical research company, Jack spent most of his day working in a separate room at the back of a large lab. Without offering reasons or excuses, Jack admitted to eventually filling empty glass containers with whiskeys of any strength or brand. This "cover" allowed him access to alcohol whenever he wished. And he wished it with increased frequency. Naturally, his happy marriage was happy no longer! A separation (not a divorce) was his wife's decision. As the months passed, Jack fell more deeply into the horrors of addiction. After several blacked-out days, Jack found himself in the hospital, sharing a room with an older man who was dying of wet-brain. With days to watch his room-mate dying of alcoholism, Jack's own suffering took on a spiritual as well as a physical reality. When his wife finally spelled out the bottom line for him, Jack was shaken to his soul. He had to choose between their loving relationship and his deadly addiction.

Jack paused in his story, wiped his wet cheeks, and acknowledged love's triumph. His journey back to health was a long, difficult, up-hill effort. He now lives a day at a time, and remains an active member of AA. Along with his wife, he accepts each day as a gift, as a reminder of God's faithful presence. Addictive habits of whatever intensity or duration find ways of infiltrating our everyday routines. They soon become our wants and needs. However, with prayer, insight, determination, and support, habits of renewal can replace habits of addiction.

How do we change our habits of addiction to dispositions of renewal? How do we follow Jesus' mandate to have salt in ourselves, to live at peace with each other? (Mark 9:50) We have already considered the importance of understanding the significance of change, of knowing the many faces of change, of dealing with the stress and wounds of change, of facing the fears, anxieties, and even the blessings of change. Now we can benefit from a practical consideration of a few habits that could help or hinder our personal and spiritual renewal.

The ability to develop an expanded consciousness marks us as human beings, as persons capable of thinking beyond the obvious. No sane person would argue against the importance of purposeful thinking. But too often our thinking is purposeless, Monkey-Island static, useless noise that is not easily turned off. The habit of undisciplined, unproductive "thinking" wastes an inordinate amount of time and energy. This leaves us feeling scattered, anxious, or frustrated. Habits of renewal begin with right thinking, with prayerful calmness. While focusing on our deep breathing, and by using a preferred form of the Jesus prayer, calmness can help bring us back to a more relaxed state of being. Habits of calm thinking help us to pay closer attention to what is happening now, in this present moment. Any of our routine habits can be opportunities for renewal when we make the choice to think and act in meaningful ways. But developing habits of renewal become unnecessarily difficult when we allow distractions from environmental noise to interfere with our natural need for periods of quiet time, for moments of mindfulness.

When it comes to developing habits of thinking that support our personal and spiritual renewal, we can turn to the wisdom of Scripture, to the love within our communities, to the empowerment of amazing grace. When we have the habit of right thinking, our experience of God among us becomes "electric." We feel the force of personal and spiritual renewal. The supportive embrace of this solidarity keeps us from avoiding change, from being narrow-minded. We then more readily open ourselves to God's enfolding presence, to new ways of finding meaning in both the ordinary and extraordinary happenings of each day. We find—or make—ways to connect with those who are discomforted by any kind of challenge. We learn to understand and resolve anger or impatience, and instead of negative feelings, our personal presence "vibrates" with peace, joy, and love. We can commit to speaking kindly, truthfully, and courageously.

The habit of compassion puts us in close touch with the physical and spiritual needs of ourselves, and of others. It also helps us to honor the dignity that we all have as human beings and as people of purpose. And what about the ordinary everyday habits of eating, relaxing, giving and "getting?" My early education in a parish grade school made it clear: "Giving is more blessed that receiving." However, I was never warned that this "giving" could so easily degenerate into an egocentric "power over" bad habit. Both giving and receiving, as two parts of a whole, are both essential for a generous habit. The practice of giving freely, and of receiving graciously, keeps us from an egocentricity that simply must "look good."

Eating too is another ordinary everyday habit that can carry great potential for renewal. Instead of eating hurriedly, taking time to chew thoroughly whatever we eat, adds dignity to our dining experience. It also eases the stress on our digestive system while at the same time it facilitates the absorption and assimilation of nutrients. To argue that eating has nothing to do with change and renewal is to miss the essential point altogether.

Our habits of relaxation can tell us a lot about ourselves. Knowing how to relax in body, mind, and spirit is a good habit that needs to be appreciated for the valuable practice it is. Ignorance has accused genuine relaxation of being a "waste of time," "a trick of the devil." On the contrary, when done mindfully, prayerfully, intentionally, it becomes a habit of holistic renewal, an opportunity for personal transformation. When we make the effort to develop good habits, our good habits renew us in body, mind, and spirit.

Healing Moments

1. In a quiet place, relax and breathe deeply for several seconds.
2. Bring to mind persons, places, or experiences that have helped you feel valued and genuinely happy.
3. Reflect on the self-appreciation and comfort that these persons and circumstances gave you.

4. Continue to enjoy the feeling of security, and warmth of this experience. Let this feeling flood your entire body, mind, and spirit.
5. Place your trust in the Source of all peace, love, and joy. Let your trust increase without any sense of clinging, craving, or "owning."
6. Continue your faithful practice of mindfulness, of trust in the "bigger reality." Open yourself to the blessings of change, renewal, and a holy transformation.

Empowerment Through Spiritual Practice

Before considering a few specifics about the day-to-day practice of spirituality, a brief reminder about our holistic human condition can be helpful. In the study of human biology, we find living examples of the fact that each body system operates in close conjunction with every other system. But for practical reasons, we study each system "separately." For example, the circulatory system takes us through "miles" of tubes, and millions of cells that connect with all the other tissues of the body. From start to finish, from brain to toe, and beyond, the human body's anatomy and physiology invites us to recognize the holistic "miracle" that we are. But we are more than bones, blood, and biceps. Mind and spirit inhabit, enhance, and support our human experience, and take us to the highest levels of transformative experience.

Neuroscience and spiritual practice have "buried the hatchet." They are no longer at odds with each other. In fact, they have joined forces in the search for the "good life." I have already mentioned that in his book about brain science and the biology of belief, Andrew Newberg's *Why God Won't Go Away* takes us to a deeper consideration of spirituality and our human condition, to an appreciation of our special relationship with God. Newberg gives us several valuable bits of information: experiments have linked "specific religious activities to positive psychological results; spiritual practices such as meditation, prayer, or participation in devotional services, have been shown to reduce feelings of anxiety and depression significantly, boost self-esteem, improve the quality of interpersonal relationships, and generate a more positive outlook on life." Most of us who have already experienced empowerment through spiritual practice know that the ability to connect with spiritual reality is worth the time, and the effort required. But to acknowledge that we have the capability for transcendence does not mean that we have been empowered to call the shots. No! Our part is to till the soil, to ready ourselves for God's amazing grace. We can do no more than readiness calls for. But readiness calls for a lot. It asks us to be inclusively informed, to understand and respect the complexity of life's spiritual dimension, and to adequately appreciate our own Christian path to personal and spiritual renewal.

If the core of Christian spirituality is the person, Jesus, then all the theories and practices that we know and follow as Christians must be seen as relative to him. For me, the living post-Easter Jesus is the truth I seek. It is in him that I choose to live, and move, and have my being. Jesus continues to be "the way, the truth, and the life." (John 14:16) But to "live Jesus" is a process rather than a goal. Others who also travel the Christian pilgrimage offer their compassionate, informed, and supportive help as we "process" toward Truth.

In recent years, much credit for helping to open my hesitant mind and heart to the deeper and practical meaning of God's living truth must go to Hans Kung. Although we are contemporaries in age, I did not become aware of Kung as a theological and moral leader until the Vatican II Council. He has shown me that as a Christian I must come to terms with my denominational myopia. As a concerned Christian, I ask that all constraining cords of mediaeval thinking be cut, that authoritarian Patriarchal policies be buried. In the spirit of ecumenism, I ask for understanding and respect toward religious systems that work toward global peace. Like myself, my church must cherish God's truth by appropriately adapting to the needs of change and renewal.

Another of my spiritual mentors, Karlfried Durckheim, has helped me toward personal and spiritual renewal. His supportive help directed my focus on spiritual transformation through mindfulness. *In the Way of Transformation,* he writes clearly and directly about the everyday practice of spirituality: Learn that making and drinking tea, taking a quick shower, writing a brief note, jogging in the park, listening carefully to a friend can become a spiritual practice. According to Durckheim, it is not so much our images and thoughts which are significant in our spirituality. It is our attitude! Only in an attitude of simplicity and surrender can we be "reborn," changed by grace, transformed by love. He encourages us to be open to new and unexpected ways of being conscious. He assures us that we are gifted, capable persons, created to experience Reality, to touch and to be touched by God's presence. But be cautious: This Divine Presence is not an "easy peace." It is Life, always new, often unexpected, sometimes even confusing, but forever flexible and creative. And without this vibrant inner Life, true personal and spiritual maturity never happens. This higher consciousness readies us for God's truth, for the experience of the Divine. As Durckheim puts it, "A living faith makes the believer listen to the mystery which speaks within, and always opens us further to the truth of Christ.

Being open to Durckheim's message can be enlightening for any adult, but especially for senior folks; he offers good advice, cautioning against refusing to admit to oneself and others that life's most beautiful gift at any age is spiritual renewal. Instead of moaning about sagging muscles, and other physical diminishments, the stirrings of a vibrant, empowering inner life becomes outwardly obvious; a transformational youth shines through. For those who choose to be awakened to the Truth, Durckheim sees the issue as no longer about "living and dying," but about "living and being born again."

Spiritual practice is about destiny. Our human destiny is to unfold to full possibility. This necessitates growing beyond the egocentric self to the essential Self. It means having an inclusive perspective that validates both inner (spiritual) and outer (psychological) aspects of our ordinary life. Spiritual practice is about witness: "We are a part of the divine being whose purpose is to manifest itself in us and through us." Each of us is destined to bear witness in our own special way, to God as both immanent and transcendent, to God who is beyond space, time, and ordinary understanding. Spiritual practice is about breakthrough. When disappointment, pain, or anxiety, periodically open inner wounds, we use these everyday happenings as opportunities for "inner work." If any one of us is serious about becoming the true person we are meant to be, then we must seriously consider that "The true person is one who is present in the world in the right way."

This suggests the significance of postures, gestures, and other concrete ways of being present, all of which tell the truth about us—whether we intend it or not. Any up-tightness, rigidity, or tenseness automatically reflects our neediness. On the other hand, a relaxed, direct simplicity tells the opposite tail. In order to break away from neurotic, superficial, egocentric habits, we must first recognize them, and then move beyond their strangling reaches. This takes graced effort, perhaps even a bit of professional help. The pay-off: empowerment, transformation, and the experience of our inner essence, of our connection with Divine Being. When we can humbly accept the truth of who we are, we might be visited by an experience of "being comforted far beyond the comprehension of our normal consciousness."

Spiritual practice, as Durckheim presents it, does not put emphasis on "doing." God's truth requires us, quite simply, "to allow the right thing to happen." When we can accept the fact that work on our physical nature affects our spiritual nature, and vice versa, we are ready for this "lift off," for letting go, for letting it happen. Getting the feel of this part of spirituality can be difficult. Maintaining a balance between a trustful, flexible attitude, while at the same time, keeping an active personal responsibility has the feel of a real challenge. The practice of spirituality keeps us focused on whatever we are doing at any moment of day or night. Nothing need separate us from awareness of Divine Being, of God within and beyond us.

When an inclusive, informed attitude sets the groundwork for an empowering spiritual practice, another essential step can be taken. Unfortunately, "meditation" has become one of those popular buzz words used indiscriminately by multi-media sales sharks. But serious, informed writers about spirituality have given extensive information and helpful advice on "how to meditate." Although I am among the grateful living who have gained much from such guidance, I must admit that theoretical expertise did not help much when I sat to meditate. Theoretical know-how has its value, but it often misses the mark when it comes to calming a mind caught up in the habits of Monkey Island's mindless shenanigans. After trying various "rules" for gaining mind-control, and after finding that, for me, they had minimal—or no—effect, I opted for common sense and my own home-grown, and not necessarily original, approach to meditation. The change was rewarding.

For starters, I developed the habit of saving approximately fifteen minutes twice a day for quiet solitude. I used an undisturbed corner of the house. There, I sat up-right in a relaxed position, focusing on my breathing-in and breathing-out. Using my preferred mantra ("Jesus," and "loving God," I tried to give my attention to God's presence within and beyond me. Too soon, attention can stray to worrisome concerns about "How will I pay this month's bills? "How serious is Dad's heart condition?" Don't be discouraged. Simply ask what this disquietude is trying to say. Usually, a Medusa head of security and control needs surface. When the truth of this neediness sinks deeply into mind and heart, then go back to deep breathing and the chosen mantra prayer. Finally, the most difficult part: practicing this inward discipline faithfully. Nothing dramatic ever happens. Perhaps a slight increase in more kindly thoughts, in more caring behavior may become evident. But nothing to write home about! And yet, little things mean a lot, especially slight increases in more kindly thoughts, in greater patience, enthusiasm, and joy in relationship with self and others. And God? A wordless, close encounter like no other kind!

It has become very clear to me that transformative spirituality involves continual change, on-going development in thoughts, attitudes, feelings, values, and behaviors. As far as "progress" is concerned, simply forget it. Admittedly, it takes some doing, but learn to relax, and wait. Know that within the self lies the answer to our meaningful quest. We need to learn how to be inwardly quiet, and to let our expanded awareness have its way. Whatever else this approach to the spiritual life suggests, the emphasis is not on dawn-to-dusk sacrifices, nor is it primarily about being a card-carrying church-goer. It is about opening ourselves to God, who is in fact already present within us.

A practical warning: Ideals can be especially troublesome when they entice us into believing that we can win God's approval by doing things perfectly. God's love asks only that we appreciate and use our unique capabilities, that we let go of knitted-brow intensity. As Wilkie Au reminds us in *The Way of the Heart*, not only book learning, but our own trials and errors can help us toward personal and spiritual transformation. All our experiences, including mistakes and failures, can help to keep our ideals in proper perspective.

Then, eventually, we can experience the personal empowerment that spiritual practice allows.

Healing Moments

1. Find a quiet place. Sit alone, and breathe deeply and gently.
2. Be sensitive to the Invisible Presence that is with you always.
3. Consider you Model, Jesus whose life reflected compassion, fairness, and an attitude of gentle openhearted acceptance of everyone. How do you follow his example?
4. In Act 9:1-48, we are given the story of Peter's courage in overcoming prejudice against "outsiders." Do you tend to make excuses, or try to rationalize your prejudice for "my own kind?" How do you join Peter by following Jesus' example?
5. Again, be mindful of the Divine Presence. Continue to be relaxed and trustful of God's unconditional love.
6. In openness of mind and spirit, embrace the Truth of life's good news. Accept the challenge of change; heal your inner wounds, and learn to live in peace, love, and joy!

Revisit the Forgotten Virtues

The practice of virtuous living is not easy to come by. It often begins with a commitment to simplicity. But simplicity rarely gets good press, even though saints and scholars count it as essential to the good life. We need not apologize when considering simplicity as a core practice from which other habits of excellence stem. In the gospel (Matt 5:37) Jesus tells his disciples to keep their answers simple and direct, to give a clear "yes," or "no." Without unnecessary ifs, ands, or buts, simplicity keeps our responses spontaneous and on-target. In psychotherapeutic terminology, this straight-forward approach is sometimes referred to as relational transparency. However, by any name or definition, the habit of simplicity takes an honored place among the virtuous qualities that enhance our holistic well-being.

Simplicity prevents intellectual navel-gazing. It helps us avoid getting lost in undue introspection, through which we can too easily lose contact with reality. Simplicity teaches us how to remain unattached from everything, especially from our egocentric self. Simplicity is the great letting-go habit, without which transformative progress remains an empty ideal. When the bad times of life lead us into despondency, when the good times of life lull us into complacency, we need the common-sense virtue of simplicity with its reality-based perspective, its can-do habit of action.

Life has its own way of shaking our foundations, and dropping us squeaking and squealing into the arms of reality. We want to bask in the warmth of a comfortable assurance; we get instead the unwanted challenge of change. We expect the clarity of absolutes; we find only tantalizing "maybe." With expectations thwarted, dreams fractured, ego wounded, we limp along life's highway, hoping for a Good Samaritan to eventually come our way, and restore our womb-like complacency. Instead simplicity arrives, wakes us to a true understanding of both inward and outward reality, and admonishes us to pick ourselves up and "get on with it."

When our expectations call for Plan A to get us "on base," a curve ball comes our way. Plan B demands that we make the necessary adjustments, but while implementing Plan B, a surprise fast-ball on the inside corner gives us a called third strike, an "out." Simplicity accepts reality without worry about image or reputation. Simplicity has no hidden agenda, no contrived motives. A basic definition of simplicity might find expression in "What you see is what you get." Andre Comte-Sponville describes simplicity as both a virtue and a grace. In his *A Small Treatise on the Great Virtues*, he reminds us, "For God everything is simple; for the simple person, everything is divine—even work, and even effort." He goes on to tell how simplicity is a here-and-now virtue, and that no virtue is worth the name unless it is simple. Simplicity reminds us to forget our pride and fear, to nurture peace, joy, spontaneity, truth, and love. Simplicity stands as the virtue of wise persons, as the wisdom of saints, as the "foolishness" of Jesus.

Simplicity, the deep-rooted vine of quality living, gives life to its many virtuous extensions. For example, when generosity and courage join forces with simplicity, they present human capability at its best. As dinner parties go, Simon knew the unspoken rule: make your guests comfortable. Good food, good wine, good conversation can go a long way in making an evening with friends and acquaintances most enjoyable. In the course of free flow conversation, many of Simon's guests felt compelled to strut their grasp of local politics, religious observations, and tax mandates. By the time the serving staff cleared the table, and offered the final dinner drinks, it had become clear that a young rabbi guest firmly supported the primacy of an individual's rights and dignity. During a lull in the after-dinner chatter, an uninvited woman appeared at the side entrance. Her graceful moves caught the eyes of the all-male guests. Within a few wordless moments, she had accomplished her purpose: to carefully and deliberately pour her flask of precious perfume onto the head of Jesus. Immediately, audible whispers from the elders confirmed their unequivocal annoyance at her presence, and their strong disapproval of her "extravagance." Among all the men present, only one challenged their unkind thoughts, words, and condescending attitude.

"Why must you make her feel uncomfortable? She has done a beautiful thing." (Mark 14:6)

This generous and courageous woman rejected the accepted social customs of her day, customs that kept her and others in unjust bondage. She opted for change. She chose to go beyond small-mindedness, prejudice, arrogance. Mindful of her inner directives, she anointed Jesus' head with her precious perfume. Now, over twenty centuries after that first Wednesday of Holy Week encounter, women are still stepping forward with simplicity's courage and generosity. This week's mail brought me the true story of a grandmother, mother, and adult daughter (all the same family) who continue to support the autonomy and dignity of women worldwide. By their generosity, by their courageous stand against unquestioning prejudice, by their firm position against women-as-minor-gender, they are models of virtuous living. When simplicity shows its generous and courageous habits of virtue, it often looks like heroism, justice, and compassion, all woven together in the priceless fabric of human excellence. Living in the spirit of simplicity opens us to the blessings of creative change, to the opportunities for personal and spiritual renewal.

Compassion can be justifiably described as an egalitarian virtue, a habit of human concern for the suffering of all living creatures. Compassion makes no value judgments, serves both those we admire, and those whose behavior we disapprove. When understood as unconditional kindness toward all life, including one's own, compassion becomes a key to lasting joy. It allows a capacity for great patience, for keeping a positive attitude, especially when the winds of change shake the foundations of our contentment. Compassion helps us to be mindful, open, and understanding of suffering, even when hurt comes to us from the malevolent behavior of others.

According to both Christian and Zen Buddhist perspectives on compassion, my neighbor is myself; consequently, my service to others must be as natural and spontaneous as the in-and-out rhythms of my breathing. When Jesus told us to love our enemies, he was not asking us to do the impossible. He was expecting us to look closely and deeply into the formative sources of the hateful behavior that causes so much pain. These mindful insights can change, and transform our anger into compassion; they can bring us to wanting the well-being of those who hurt themselves and others.

Our North American culture is known for being very individualistic. Colonial history of the United States does not lack its heroic tales of folks who wagoned their way up, down, and across the many miles of unexplored land in order to help establish the first democratic nation of its kind. Few would dispute the blessings of this distinctive style of independent thinking and acting. For more than political, social, economic, educational, and religious reasons, individual determination made its contribution to democratic living, to human well-being. But mavericks, loners, free spirits are not the whole story of individual accomplishments. Because, as human beings, we are relational, compassionate caring for each other remains an essential virtue. In Robert Kennedy's eloquent book, *Zen Gifts to Christians*, he mentions a young Jewish woman, Etty Hillesum, who was captured by the Nazis in Holland in 1943. While still in the Westerbork camp, she wrote that at night she would listen, as she lay on her plank bed, to the other women and girls sobbing, tossing and turning, wanting not to think or feel, for fear that they would surely go out of their minds. She felt filled with tender compassion, and lay awake for hours, praying that she might be the compassionate heart of the whole concentration camp. For Etty Hillesum this meant turning away from hatred, and living in love. Why? Etty wrote, "It has been brought home forcibly to me here, how every atom of hatred added to the world makes it an even more inhospitable place." By the same logic, every service of compassionate love makes the world a better place. When we become keenly aware of our connections, of our "human bondage," compassionate concern can enrich our lives, and those of others.

The Dalai Lama has said, "There is no secret method by which compassion and loving kindness can come about." We must learn to thoughtfully, prayerfully, patiently, perseveringly attend to our holistic, developmental life changes. Unless we work toward enlightened compassion, our "spirituality" is questionable; it has the sound of "tinkling symbols." From a psychospiritual perspective, only when we learn to nurture ourselves, to care for "our inner child," to get beyond egotistical attitudes, to have compassion for self and other, only then can we make our way beyond hurtful impulses and desires. When doubts and difficulties challenge us, Saint Paul's words make clear that love is always patient and kind; love is never boastful or conceited; it is never rude or selfish; it takes no offense, and is not resentful. Love delights in truth, and endures whatever comes. (1 Cor. 13:4-7)

Although not the first to do so, Sogyal Rinpoche, in *The Tibetan Book of Living and Dying*, cautions that before practicing compassion toward others, I must first practice compassion toward myself. This can be difficult for those of us who see ourselves as deficient in value, and wanting in those qualities which our culture deems most desirable. Physical beauty, mental quickness, financial "big bucks" are not available simply for the asking. Being left with a plain appearance, average comprehensive ability, and a thin bank account, our options for popular attention are limited. But perhaps this is a blessing in disguise, an opportunity to evoke compassion within and for ourselves.

Rinpoche suggests that in opening ourselves to this inward, self-compassion, we begin by going back into our personal history. He suggests that we remember someone (relative, mentor, significant other, whose love for us, we felt vividly. In my own case, when I was tempted to feel depressingly unworthy, I learned to tap into early childhood memories of my dear Uncle Ted. To be exact, he was my Dad's favorite uncle, therefore, my great-uncle. He was the man I fell totally in love with at the age of four. Now, in my older years, vivid memory allows me still to bath in the warmth of his unconditional, enfolding love. The free flow of that shared affection fills me with gratitude, with the realization that I am worthy of love, that I am in fact lovable. When this remembered goodness expands to the realization of God's unending love, compassion overflows as a healing balm over all hurts. When we free ourselves from the strangle-hold of disaffection for self, then compassion can move more freely, more surely to mend painful wounds.

In his compassion for Jerusalem, Jesus likened himself to a mother-hen gathering, protecting her chicks within the warm embrace of her feathered wings. (Matt. 23:37-39) It would be difficult to find any section of the gospel that does not give some evidence of the compassionate actions of Jesus. In Mark 8:1-2, he says, "I have compassion for the crowd because they have been with me now for three days and have nothing to eat." In John 11:33, Martha and Mary have lost their brother Lazarus; he is dead. When Jesus saw Mary weeping, and the Jews who came with her weeping, he was greatly disturbed in spirit, and deeply moved. At this point, Jesus' compassion leads directly to his action. And so with us too, our compassionate thoughts and feelings must lead to agency, whether it be physical, mental, spiritual, or all of the above.

Justice is defined by Aristotle as a complete virtue because according to him, it is the precondition for humane, righteous behavior. If we try to excuse unjust actions by suggesting they are motivated by love or caring, then we are not, in fact, talking about either love or caring, but rather about favoritism, partiality. Anytime we excuse unjust behavior under the pretext that it is the price of happiness, then selfishness results. Without real justice, all our values, all our virtues are counterfeit. Since the essentials of justice include freedom for everyone, respect for the dignity and right of every individual, then "morality and justice came before legality." When we tap into the political history of our USA, we find a most challenging narrative wrapped around issues of race, gender, and religion—to mention only a few. Morris Dee's biography, *A Lawyer's Journey*, tells of his life-long work to extend the influence of justice until as the Biblical prophet Amos says, "Justice rolls down like waters." Through his years of fighting injustice, Dees "learned that we can never fear the consequences of standing up to hate. And we can never be indifferent to acts of injustice." We must work for change.

Since we carry the seeds of injustice within egocentric, self-centered attitudes, it is necessary to know the faces of our enemies: intolerance, prejudice. Returning again to Andre Comte-Sponville's work on the great virtues, we are reminded: To tolerate an injustice of which we are not a victim, to tolerate an atrocity of which we are spared is not tolerance, but gross indifference, hateful selfishness. This kind of unlimited tolerance would be the end of tolerance. Like "birds of a feather," intolerance, fanaticism, and dogmatism all hang together, doing damage wherever they go. By contrast, tolerance is broad-based wisdom that readily overcomes any distortions of truth. Comte-Sponville points out that intolerance makes people stupid just as stupidity makes people intolerant.

When dogmatism leads to complacency, exclusion, and contempt of others, then intolerance is close by. Gone are the days when the Church could have Giordano Bruno burned at the stake. Deo gratias! Whether in philosophical, theological, psychological, or everyday language, tolerance is a virtue that stands against fanaticism, sectarianism, authoritarianism, or any other form of intolerance, or any attitude of prejudice. Tolerance stands for justice.

Perhaps no one has explored the issue of prejudice as thoroughly as G.W. Allport who gives us good reason to take a close look at Peter's challenge against intolerance. In Acts 9:1-48, we are given the story of Peter, his associates, and the issue of prejudice. The very early days of the Church were understandably confusing for its leadership, especially concerning the acceptance of new members. Were the followers of Jesus to consider themselves a new chapter in Judaism? Were outsiders, called gentiles, to be included? In those formative years of the New Testament Church, Jews were very prejudiced against non-Jews. Even Peter and the other disciples of Jesus tended to express their anti-gentile convictions. But soon the Holy Spirit had a say against the prejudicial behavior.

At one point in Peter's missionary journeys, he met the Italian centurion, Cornelius, who being a religious person, wanted to know more about the ideas and practices of Christianity. So he sent a message to Peter, requesting a visit. This threw Peter into great conflict: Jews were forbidden to socialize with "outsiders." But Jesus showed concern and compassion to all outcasts! Shortly after Cornelius' message reached him, Peter had fallen asleep and dreamed that out of the heavens came a huge sheet on which all kinds of four-footed animals were seen. When Peter heard a voice telling him to eat these creatures, Peter said, "No way!" According to Jewish protocol, he had never eaten "unclean" food and was not about to begin. Then a voice admonished Peter that the food he refused to eat was not unclean. So with cautious hesitation, Peter visited Cornelius, preached to him and his household, and baptized each person. But when Peter returned to Jerusalem, he faced his scandalized associates who insisted that Jesus' good news was only for the in-group. Peter stood his ground, pointing out that gentiles belong to God too. Eventually, they saw "the bigger picture," and joined Peter in his praise of God for this significant change in early Church policy.

This gospel incident exemplifies the natural tendency we all have toward prejudiced behavior, toward making generalizations that over-simplify real life experiences. Like Peter, we sometimes allow our personal preferences to predispose us toward making false judgments that can easily lead to intolerant behavior. Even today, anti-feminism, as expressed in ancient as well as recent dogmatic statements by some Church authorities, gives clear evidence of denigration and gross over-generalization, both of which are basic ingredients of prejudice.

Revisiting the less-famous virtues of simplicity, compassion, and justice reminds us again to heed Jesus' teaching moment in which he urges us to have the salt of renewal within ourselves, and to live at peace with each other. (Mark 9:50)

Spiritual Flourishing

Is it true that too many persons live lives of quiet desperation? From my personal perspective as a psychotherapist and educator, I would have to say "no" to the quiet, and "yes" to the desperation. Some live in frenetic activity at one extreme; some experience depressive stupor at the other. The in-between ways of living appear more or less "desperate" depending on one's openness to the challenges of change and renewal, and to the opportunities for holistic flourishing.

For many of us, flourishing conjures up images of self-indulgence, of narcissism, of "doing your thing." Add to this misconception the remnants of mediaeval ideologies that stressed personal sinfulness, and exaggerated unworthiness. The result? An over-valuation of "penance" and "discipline!" The truth of the matter is that flourishing is a positive force, an essential, virtuous practice in any meaningful life.

In her volume, *The Fragility of Goodness*, Martha Nussbaum gives a direct understanding of flourishing. She reminds us that for the Greeks, flourishing meant that a person was living a good life, being a beneficent presence to self, and to others. It meant thriving rather than simply surviving! Human flourishing depends largely on the decisions we choose to make. It gives us a mandate to listen deeply to our own story, to recognize the real limits of our human efforts, to avoid any form of extremism that might inhibit the full development of our personal and spiritual well-being.

In his humanity, Jesus gave us a perfect model of a flourishing life. He showed us what it means to thrive. By his own lived example he has shown us how to "be alert," how to expand our consciousness, how to grasp the implications of our having "the kingdom of God" within us. The work of spiritual flourishing is truly the work of waking up to "God with us." Jesus put a lot of time and energy into sharing the "good news," into encouraging us to wake-up, to flourish, to rejoice. In Luke 8:49-56, a little girl's parents were astonished when Jesus called the child to wake up. So too he calls each of us to wake up, to flourish, to rejoice, and to attend more consciously to what it means to be truly alive.

Our flourishing as human persons must include faithful attention to God's presence within, among, and beyond us. But most of us "are concerned about many things." Our commitment to our spiritual flourishing remains second-rate, something to consider *if* time and circumstances allow. We often spend an inordinate amount of time focusing on "doing good." Doing good works is, of course, praiseworthy, but it can also feed an egocentric mind-set. Being good is a much more difficult, egoless way of life. Being good more directly identifies the flourishing life, a life that reflects clearly the Christian message of courage, love, peace, and joy.

Jesus supports the fullness of life which has little or nothing to do with wealth, power, prestige, or "success." When Saint Paul tells us to take Christ inside ourselves (Rm. 13-14), he wants us to attend to our interior "being," to our flourishing. He wants us to be mindful of the dignity that is ours, regardless of any "accomplishments."

Possessions and material stuff do not necessarily impede or advance our personal or spiritual flourishing. But extremes of either poverty or wealth can easily interfere with our thriving life. To put more effort into gaining possessions, or into glorifying poverty, misses the mark entirely. When we listen to, and live faithfully God's word, we begin to flourish. In *Breakthrough*, by Matthew Fox, he comments on Meister Eckhart's thought: "The word spoken from God's spirit to my spirit is truly a fruitful word, and a word of awakening and resurrection. It is a word that is barely a whisper, but it can be heard by those who listen and keep it." Yes, we flourish when we hear God's word and keep it.

Jesus did not use the word "flourishing." But in a different choice of words he spoke about living a vigorous, productive, mindful life: "You must have salt in yourselves, and live at peace with each other." (Mark 9:50) We might ask ourselves what are the marks of a flourishing person? What are a few indications that an individual is thriving, is being "salt of the earth?"

Being open to continuous human growth is an essential characteristic of a person who is committed to living fully the spiritual dimension of life. But living the fullness of life includes the struggles and challenges of various kinds of change. Without these experiences, our spirituality might be superficial, without solid foundation.

Mistakes happen! When they do, it is a great advantage when they lead to the correction of faulty notions. In the course of my early adult life, I made a huge developmental mistake. I erroneously concluded that spiritual maturity had little to do with human psychosocial development. I wrongly believed that grace could be a substitute for nature, when in fact it fulfills nature. My simplistic perspective led me to the either/or distortion of a complex reality, of what true flourishing is about.

These and similar mistakes or confusions about personal and spiritual renewal find remedy in the regular practice of meditation. The aficionados of all major world religions assure us that meditative awareness is a quintessential quality of spirituality. In helping us to understand and honor our human dignity, meditation also sets in motion the realization that every part of life, including everyday happenings, and unexpected challenges, are opportunities to experience close contact with Reality, to live a flourishing life. And to help others do the same!

Openness to the challenges and blessings of change allows personal and spiritual renewal to happen. This willingness to change our minds and hearts, to live the good news, calls us to value silence and prayerful "inwardness," to appreciate the connection between our everyday reality and God's timeless reality. Because the flourishing of human beings involves both secular and sacred, both nature and grace, any denial of this holistic reality distorts and confuses what it means to be fully alive. But fullness of life does not just happen. It requires a firm commitment to our evolving, on-going personal development—including the vitally important, yet often ignored, spiritual dimension.

From a psychological perspective, when we relate to life with an expansive consciousness, with a broad-based awareness, and when we are not caught in the trap of a rigid mind-set, then we are capable of the most profound religious experiences. Choosing to live deliberately, mindfully in the present moment, no matter what it brings, enables us to absorb and radiate that powerful energy of the Divine Presence. This is the source of creative living, of enhanced well-being, of spiritual transformation. This is why personal and spiritual renewal is so essential to living life fully.

Thoughtful consideration of how to make wiser life-change decisions, and how to flourish in body, mind, and spirit, gives us good reason to rejoice. We are then better able to understand more thoroughly, and to heal more completely our inner wounds of change, transition, and loss. We can now more resolutely accept God's gracious invitation to live life fully, to experience holistic renewal, and to be the salt of the earth.

Reflective Moments

1. What is your understanding of simplicity? Why is it a very significant virtue in our present global culture?

2. Characteristics of all flourishing, healthy life include a vigorous, receptive, enthusiastic quality. In what ways do you understand Jesus' gospel message to live life fully, and to believe his good news?
3. Habits of calm thinking, feeling, and acting, help us to clearly discern what is happening in the present moment. To what extent are you habitually able to be mindful? What are you willing to do in order to increase your mindfulness of the Divine Presence?
4. If you choose to live the fullness of life each day, how do you go about living that fullness as you eat, shower, exercise, converse, work, and so on?
5. In the practice of personal and spiritual renewal, how have your own trials and errors helped you to keep your ideal in proper perspective, so that ideals do not become troublesome idols?
6. When understood as unconditional kindness, compassion can become a key to peace, joy, and love. How do you practice compassionate and positive attitudes toward yourself, so that you may be the "salt of the earth?" (Mark 9:50)

EPILOGUE

We know that facing the challenges of life's many changes is not an option. We also know that how we go about encountering any unwelcome happenings is clearly our choice. The question life puts to us is clear: Will we take full advantage of life's unexpected challenges and expand our consciousness, gain personal empowerment? Or will we let valuable moments of possibility pass us by as we go mindlessly through our days. Will we miss the many opportunities for our renewal, peace, and joy?

In today's frenetic lifestyle, time for quiet, creative insights rarely finds entry into our daily schedules. Who would argue against our need for "down time?" Without it we can hardly enjoy deeper understanding and purposeful action. Without quiet moments it is inconceivable that our enhanced, holistic well-being can become reality.

The quiet moments that allowed your reading through these pages can help you become more keenly aware of several basic facts and practical suggestions which can, in turn, lead to the resolution of life's change-challenges. Your decision to learn more about personal and spiritual renewal is significant. Why? Because the practical information shared here is directly related to the Great Commandment (Mark 12:28-34). Your understanding, acceptance, and healing of change, transition, and loss wounds increases your ability to flourish, to live life fully, and to help others do the same. "I came that they might have life, and that they might have it more abundantly." (John 10:10)

Unhealed wounds do to our mind, feelings, and spirit what wounds do in very obvious ways to our bodies. They cut down on our enthusiasm, energy, joy. In extreme cases, unattended wounds fester, spread their pain, and cause unnecessary misery. Unattended wounds of any kind cause suffering to the whole person. We have learned—and are still learning—about the holistic nature of human life. Unlike former beliefs, we now have ample proof of our body, mind, spirit, of our unified nature. As humans, we function systemically. We are a unified whole. There is no place for dualism here in the flourishing personality.

Critical comments might warn of narcissism, of too much focus on the self. If this is the impression of an honest reader, I sincerely apologize for not being clear on this point. Let me say now that narcissistic tendencies, or any other neurotic tendencies, have no part in the healing process of any personal, spiritual wounds. In simple terms, "You cannot give what you do not have!" If you have not dealt effectively with your own inner wounds of change, transition, and loss you will never be able effectively to help others meet and resolve their inner wounds. Many centuries ago, Augustine prayed that he might know God, that he might know himself. The truth of self-understanding is God's truth. Psychospiritual truth leads us to personal and spiritual renewal—for ourselves, for others.

Many of us, committed to psychospiritual flourishing, consider Thomas Merton as a postmodern spiritual aficionado. He lived his too short life totally dedicated to God and others. I remember being deeply touched by his conviction that in our communal worship of God, we must each bring the gift of our individual, spiritual life to share with others. And he reminds us through his writings to steer clear of false spirituality. This is the kind of practice that is empty of any deep inner awakening, and is marked by a dependence on those externals that rob us of freedom and peace. This counterfeit practice gives authentic inwardness bad press. A common but ignorant accusation sees spirituality as something one "gets." But the truth is that real spirituality is about our giving of ourselves—as Jesus did!

In these pages we have seen that flourishing of human persons involves both the "secular and the sacred," both nature and grace, both psychology and spirituality. When we deny this holistic reality, we distort and confuse what it means to be fully alive. And yes, this fullness requires a commitment to our own evolving psychological and spiritual development. It requires that we make an honest effort to heal all our inner wounds, that we value an expansive consciousness, and avoid any rigid, narrow mindset.

I hope I have helped to encourage you to understand, to value your dignity as a human person, as an "imago Dei." In spite of—perhaps even because of—our many wounds of change, each of us can resolve to bring healing to ourselves and others. We can resolve to share with those around us the fruits of our personal and spiritual renewal.

Although this reading is finished, our holistic growth and development is on-going. Let us continue to flourish in body, mind, and spirit! May we inspire each other to move forward in peace, love, and joy!

BIBLIOGRAPHY

Allport, Gordon. *The Individual and His Religion.* Collier-Macmillan, 1969.
_____ *The Nature of Prejudice.* Addison-Wesley Publishing Co., 1979.
Anderson, Ray. *Theology, Death, and Dying.* Basil Blackwell, Ltd., 1986.
Armstrong, Karen. *The Great Transformation: The Beginning of our Religious Traditions.* Alfred A. Knopf, 2006.
_____ *Twelve Steps to a Compassionate Life.* Random House, Inc., 2010.
Au, Wilkie. *By Way of the Heart: Toward a Holistic Christian Spirituality.* Paulist Press, 1989.
Barzun, Jacques. *A Stroll With William James.* University of Chicago Press, 1983.
Blackman, Douglas. *Slavery By Another Name.* Anchor Books, 2009.
Blakney, Raymond. *Meister Eckhart: A Modern Translation.* Harper and Row, 1941.
Borg, Marcus, and Crosson, John D. *The Last Week.* Harper Collins Publisher, 2006.
Bowlby, John. *Separation: Anxiety and Anger.* Basic Books, Inc., Publishers, 1973.
_____ *Loss: Sadness and Depression.* Harper Collins Publisher, 1980.
Bradshaw, John. *Healing the Shame that Binds You.* Health Communications, Inc., 1988.
Brauch, Manfred. *Abusing Scripture: The Consequences of Misreading the Bible.* InterVarsity Press, 2009.
Bridges, William. *Transitions: Making Sense of Life's Changes.* Addison-Wesley Publishing Co., Inc. 1980.
Brodie, Richard. *Virus of the Mind: The New Science of the Meme.* Hay House, Inc., 1996.
Bruner, Jerome. *The Culture of Education.* Harvard University Press, 1996.
Campbell, Joseph. *The Power of Myth: with Bill Moyers.* Doubleday, 1988.
Carr, Anne. *A Search for Wisdom and Spirit: Thomas Merton's Theology of the Self.* University of Notre Dame Press, 1998.

Coles, Robert. *The Spiritual Life of Children*. Houghton Mifflin, 1990.
Comte-Sponville, A. *A Small Treatise on the Great Virtues*. Henry Holt and Co., 2001.
Conn, J. W. *Spirituality and Personal Maturity*. Paulist Press, 1989.
Damasio, A. *Descartes' Error: Emotion, Reason, and the Human Brain*. Harper Collins, 1994.
_____ *The Feeling of What Happens: Body and Emotion in the Making of Consciousness*. Harcourt, Inc., 1999.
_____ *Looking for Spinoza: Joy, Sorrow, and the Feeling Brain*. Harcourt, Inc., 2003.
Dees, Morris. *A Lawyer's Journey*. American Bar Association, 2001.
DeSales, Francis. *Treatise on the Love of God*. Doubleday, 1963.
Durckheim, Karlfried. *The Way of Transformation: Daily Life as Spiritual Practice*. Morning Light Press, 2007.
Eliade, Marcea. *The Sacred and the Profane*. Harper and Row Publishers, 1961.
Elie, Paul. *The Life You Save May Be Your Own*. Farror, Straus, and Giroux, 2003.
Finley, James. *Merton's Place of Nowhere*. Ave Maria Press, 1978.
Fowler, James. *The Stages of Faith: The Psychology of Human Development and the Quest for Meaning*. Harper Collins, 1981.
Frame, M. *Integrating Religion and Spirituality into Counseling*. Brooks/Cole, 2003.
Frankl, Viktor. *Man's Search for Ultimate Meaning*. Perseus Publishing, 2000.
_____ *The Will To Meaning*. Teachers College Press, 1969.
Furlong, Monica. *Merton: A Biography*. Harper and Row Publishers, Inc., 1981.
Fiorenza, Elizabeth Schussler. *Discipleship of Equals*. Crossroad Publishing Co., 1993.
_____ *In Memory of Her*. Crossroad Publishing Co., 1985.
_____ *Searching the Scriptures*. Crossroad Publishing Co., 1997.
_____ *Sharing Her Word*. Beacon Press, 1998.
Fox, Mathew. *Breakthrough: Meister Eckhart's Creation Spirituality*. Doubleday, Inc., 1980.
Gilbert, Paul. *The Compassionate Mind*. New Harbinger Publications, Inc., 2009.
Goldberg, Elkonan. *The Executive Brain: Frontal Lobes and the Civilized Mind*. Oxford University Press, 2001.
Grant, Terrance. *The Silence of Unknowing*. Triumph Books, 1995.
Gratton, Carolyn. *The Art of Spiritual Guidance*. Crossroad Publishing Co., 1997.

Guitton, Jean. *The Spiritual Genius of Saint Therese of Lisieux.* Triumph Books, 1997.
Hahn, Tich Nhat. *Living Buddha, Living Christ.* Riverhead Books, 1995.
_____ *Touching Peace.* Parallax Press, 1992.
_____ *Peace Is Every Step: The Path of Mindfulness in Everyday Life.* Bantam Books, 1991.
Hall, Stephen. *Wisdom: From Philosophy to Neuroscience.* Vintage Books, 2010.
Hartshorne, Charles. *Omnipotence and Other Theological Mistakes.* State University of New York Press, 1984.
Higgins, John. *Thomas Merton On Prayer.* Doubleday and Co., 1975.
Horney, Karen. *Neurosis and Human Growth.* W. W. Norton and Co., Inc., 1950.
_____ *Our Inner Conflicts: A Constructive Theory of Neurosis.* W. W. Norton and Co., Inc., 1945.
_____ *Self Analysis.* W. W. Norton and Company, Inc. 1994.
James, Henry. "Washington Square" in *Great Short Works of Henry James.* Harper and Row Publishers, 1966.
James, William. *The Varieties of Religious Experience.* Crowell-Collier Publishing Co., 1961.
_____ *The Will To Believe, and Human Immortality.* Dover Publications, Inc., 1956.
Johnson, Elizabeth. *She Who Is: The Mystery of God in Feminist Theological Discourse.* Crossroad Publishing Co., 1996.
Jung, Carl G. *Psychology and Religion.* Yale University Press, 1938.
_____ *Modern Man in Search of a Soul.* Harcourt, Brace, Jovanovich Publishers, 1933.
Kabot-Zinn, Jon. *Full Catastrophe Living.* Random House, Inc., 1990.
Kavanaugh, K. and Rodriguez, O. *The Collected Works of St. John of the Cross.* ICS Publications, 1979.
Kegan, Robert. *The Evolving Self: Problem and Process in Human Development.* Harvard University Press, 1982.
Kennedy, Robert. *Zen Gifts to Christians.* Continuum International Publishing Group, Inc., 2000.
_____ *Zen Spirit, Christian Spirit.* Continuum International Publishing Group, Inc., 1995.
Kluger, Richard. *Simple Justice.* Alfred Knopf Inc., 1975.
Kubler-Ross, Elizabeth. *On Death and Dying.* Macmillan Publishing Co. Inc., 1979.
Kung, Hans. *Great Christian Thinkers.* Continuum Publishing Co., 1996.
_____ *Truthfulness: The Future of the Church.* Sheed and Ward, Inc., 1968.
_____ *The Catholic Church: A Short History.* Random House, Inc., 2001.

_____ *My Struggle For Freedom*. W. B. Eerdmans Publishing Co., 2003.
_____ *Women In Christianity*. Continuum Publishing Co., 2005.
_____ *Credo: The Apostles' Creed Explained for Today*. Doubleday, Inc., 1993.
_____ *Dying with Dignity: A Plea for Personal Responsibility*. Continuum Publishing, 1998.
_____ *The Church Maintained In Truth: A Theological Meditation*. Vintage Books, 1982.
LaCugna, Catherine, edit. *Freeing Theology*. Harper Collins Publishers, Inc., 1993.
Lama, Dalai. *Ethics For A New Millennium*. Riverhead Books, 1999.
_____ *An Open Heart*. Little, Brown Co., 2001.
LeDoux, Joseph. *The Emotional Brain: The Mysterious Underpinnings of Emotional Life*. Simon and Schuster, Inc., 1996.
Levine, Steven. *Meeting At The Edge*. Anchor Press, 1984.
Lipton, Bruce. *The Biology of Belief: Unleashing the Power of Consciousness, Matter, and Miracles*. Hay House, Inc., 2005.
Llewelyn, Robert, edit., *Julian, Woman of Our Day*. Twenty-Third Publishers, 1987.
Lopez, Steve. *Soloist*. G. P. Putnam and Sons, 2010.
Loyola, Ignatius. *The Spiritual Exercises*. Doubleday Publishing Co., 1964.
MacCullich, Diarmaid. *The Reformation: A History*. Penguin Group, Inc., 2003.
McCown, Joe. *Availability: Gabriel Marcel and the Phenomenology of Human Openness*. Scholars Press, 1984.
McGinn, Meyendorff, Leclercq, edit. *Christian Spirituality*. Crossroad Publishing Co., 1997.
Meier, John. *The Marginal Jew, Vol. III*. Random House, Inc., 2001.
_____ *The Marginal Jew. Vol. IV*. Yale University Press, 2009.
Merton, Thomas. *The Inner Experience*. Harper Collins, 2003.
_____ *New Seeds of Contemplation*. New Directions Publishing Co., 1961.
_____ *Zen and the Birds of Appetite*. New Directions Publishing Co., 1968.
_____ *Contemplation in a World of Action*. University of Notre Dame Press, 1998.
_____ *Love and Living*. Bantam Books, Inc., 1980.
_____ *The Way of Chuang Tzu*. New Directions Publishing Co., 1965.
Mitchell, K. and Anderson, H. *All Our Losses, All Our Gains*. Westminister Press, 1983.
Modras, Ronald. *Ignatian Humanism: A Dynamic Spirituality for the 21st Century*. Loyola Press, 2004.
Mott, Michael. *The Seven Mountains of Thomas Merton*. Houghton Mifflin Co., 1984.

Needleman, Jacob. *Why Can't We Be Good?* Penguin Group, Inc., 2007.
_____ *The Heart of Philosophy.* Harper Collins Publishers, 1982.
Newberg, Andrew. *Why God Won't Go Away.* Ballantine Publishing Group, 2001.
Nouwen, Henri. *The Wounded Healer.* Doubleday, Inc., 1979.
Nussbaum, Martha. *The Fragility of Goodness.* Cambridge University Press, 2001.
_____ *The Therapy of Desire.* Princeton University Press, 1994.
Ochs, Carol. *Women and Spirituality.* Rowman and Littlefield Publishers, Inc., 1997.
O'Murcha, Diarmuid. *Reclaiming Spirituality.* Crossroad Publishing Co., 1999.
Otto, Rudolph. *The Idea of the Holy.* Penguin Books, Ltd., 1959.
Pascal, Rene. *Pensees.* Penguin Putnam, Inc. 1995.
Patrick, Anne. *Liberating Conscience.* Continuum Publishing Co., 1997.
Pearce, Joseph. *The Biology of Transcendence.* Park Street Press, 2001.
Rahner, Karl. *The Practice of Faith.* Crossroad Publishing Co., 1986.
Rinpoche, Sogyal. *The Tibetan Book of Living and Dying.* Harper Collins Publishers, Inc., 1992.
Sanders, Catherine. *Grief the Mourning After.* John Wiley Sons, Inc., 1999.
Sheldrake, Philip. *Spirituality and History.* Orbis Books, 1995.
Schillebeeckx, Eduard. *Jesus.* Crossroad Publishing Co., 1979.
Siegel, Daniel. *The Developing Mind.* Guilford Press, 1999.
Smith, Huston. *Why Religion Matters.* Harper Collins Publisher, Inc., 2001.
_____ *The World's Religions.* HarperCollins Publisher, Inc., 1991.
Tillich, Paul. *Love, Power, and Justice.* Oxford University Press, 1954.
_____ *Morality and Beyond.* Westminister John Knox Press, 1963.
Tolle, Eckhart. *The Power of Now: A Guide to Spiritual Enlightenment.* New World Library, 2004.
Tolstoy, Leo. "The Death of Ivan Ilych" in *Great Short Works of Leo Tolstoy.* Harper and Row, Publishers, 1967.
Walsh, F. and McGoldrick M. *Living Beyond Loss.* W. W. Norton and Co., 1991.
Watts, Alan. *The Wisdom of Insecurity.* Random House, Inc., 1951.
Welwood, John, edit. *Ordinary Magic: Everyday Life as Spiritual Path.* Shambhala Publications, Inc., 1992.
Whitehead, Alfred N. *Adventures of Ideas.* Macmillan Co., 1933.
_____ *Science and the Modern World.* The Free Press, 1925.
Winnicott, D. W. *Home Is Where We Start From.* W. W. Norton Co., 1986.
Wolff, Robert. *Original Wisdom.* Inner Traditions, 2001.

CPSIA information can be obtained at www.ICGtesting.com
Printed in the USA
BVOW080328311012

304275BV00001B/51/P